AF745163

Social Media and Machine Learning

Edited by Alberto Cano

Published in London, United Kingdom

IntechOpen

Supporting open minds since 2005

Social Media and Machine Learning
http://dx.doi.org/10.5772/intechopen.78089
Edited by Alberto Cano

Contributors
Leila Kerkeni, Keiko Tsujioka, Alberto Cano, Setareh Majidian, Iman Raeesi Vanaei, Anil Kumar

© The Editor(s) and the Author(s) 2020
The rights of the editor(s) and the author(s) have been asserted in accordance with the Copyright, Designs and Patents Act 1988. All rights to the book as a whole are reserved by INTECHOPEN LIMITED. The book as a whole (compilation) cannot be reproduced, distributed or used for commercial or non-commercial purposes without INTECHOPEN LIMITED's written permission. Enquiries concerning the use of the book should be directed to INTECHOPEN LIMITED rights and permissions department (permissions@intechopen.com).
Violations are liable to prosecution under the governing Copyright Law.

Individual chapters of this publication are distributed under the terms of the Creative Commons Attribution 3.0 Unported License which permits commercial use, distribution and reproduction of the individual chapters, provided the original author(s) and source publication are appropriately acknowledged. If so indicated, certain images may not be included under the Creative Commons license. In such cases users will need to obtain permission from the license holder to reproduce the material. More details and guidelines concerning content reuse and adaptation can be found at http://www.intechopen.com/copyright-policy.html.

Notice
Statements and opinions expressed in the chapters are these of the individual contributors and not necessarily those of the editors or publisher. No responsibility is accepted for the accuracy of information contained in the published chapters. The publisher assumes no responsibility for any damage or injury to persons or property arising out of the use of any materials, instructions, methods or ideas contained in the book.

First published in London, United Kingdom, 2020 by IntechOpen
IntechOpen is the global imprint of INTECHOPEN LIMITED, registered in England and Wales, registration number: 11086078, 7th floor, 10 Lower Thames Street, London, EC3R 6AF, United Kingdom
Printed in Croatia

British Library Cataloguing-in-Publication Data
A catalogue record for this book is available from the British Library

Additional hard and PDF copies can be obtained from orders@intechopen.com

Social Media and Machine Learning
Edited by Alberto Cano
p. cm.
Print ISBN 978-1-78984-027-8
Online ISBN 978-1-78984-028-5
eBook (PDF) ISBN 978-1-83880-616-3

We are IntechOpen, the world's leading publisher of Open Access books

Built by scientists, for scientists

4,600+
Open access books available

119,000+
International authors and editors

135M+
Downloads

151
Countries delivered to

Our authors are among the
Top 1%
most cited scientists

12.2%
Contributors from top 500 universities

CLARIVATE ANALYTICS BOOK CITATION INDEX INDEXED

WEB OF SCIENCE™

Selection of our books indexed in the Book Citation Index
in Web of Science™ Core Collection (BKCI)

Interested in publishing with us?
Contact book.department@intechopen.com

Numbers displayed above are based on latest data collected.
For more information visit www.intechopen.com

Meet the editor

Alberto Cano is an Assistant Professor with the Department of Computer Science, Virginia Commonwealth University, USA, where he heads the High-Performance Data Mining Lab. He obtained his PhD degree in Computer Science from the University of Granada, Spain, in 2014. His research is focused on machine learning, data mining, general-purpose computing on graphics processing units, Apache Spark, and evolutionary computation. He has published over 45 articles in high-impact factor journals, made 50 contributions to conferences, two book chapters, and one book. His research is supported by an Amazon AWS Machine Learning award and the VCU Presidential Research Quest Fund. Dr Cano is an IEEE Senior Member, ACM Member, and Associate Editor of IEEE Access and Applied Intelligence.

Contents

Preface

Social media has transformed society and the way people interact with each other. The volume and speed in which new structured and unstructured content is being generated surpasses the processing capacity of traditional machine learning and data mining systems. Analyzing such data demands new approaches coming from natural language processing, text mining, sentiment analysis, big data computing, and deep learning to understand the content and resolve the arising challenges. Identification of spam, fake news, hate speech, communities, influence analysis, threats, etc. in the ever-increasing networks are among the top hot topics of machine learning and artificial intelligence in social media analytics. There is a need to develop robust, adaptable, and evolvable systems to tackle these open issues in real time in the context of the big data era and the Internet of the things, as well as to provide a meaningful and comprehensible summarization and visualization to the end users. This book provides the reader with a comprehensive overview of the latest developments in social media and machine learning, addressing research innovations, applications, trends, and open challenges in this crucial area.

Chapter 1 presents an introduction to online machine learning and data stream mining in social media. Chapter 2 presents a system for automatic speech emotion recognition using machine learning. Chapter 3 presents a case study using big data processing in education and introduces a method of matching members by optimizing collaborative learning environments. Chapter 4 presents a literature review on big data analytics that covers the extensive work in the area for the last decade. Chapter 5 presents a study on collaborative learning based on information and communication, and behavior modeling using machine learning algorithms.

Alberto Cano
Department of Computer Science,
Virginia Commonwealth University,
Richmond,
VA, USA

Chapter 1

Introductory Chapter: Data Streams and Online Learning in Social Media

Alberto Cano

1. Introduction

Since the establishment of the World Wide Web and online social media networks, people have changed the way they communicate, share experiences, and connect with each other, both in their professional and personal lives [1]. Billions of users exchange digital information on popular sites such as Facebook, Twitter, and LinkedIn but also in smaller and topic-specific networks [2, 3]. The ever-increasing number of users and content shared makes it challenging for information systems to process all the information, especially if we consider the increasing speed at which content is generated [4, 5]. Consequently, new open issues have risen regarding the effective and efficient processing of such high-speed large-scale volumes of data in online social media. How can we build machine learning systems that can handle and scale to the impressive volume of data? How can we keep a low latency in the response to classifying new real-time data? How can we classify users and their behavior? How can we early detect changes in the user's behavior and emerging trends? These are open questions to the data science scientific community [6–8].

In recent years, the design of machine learning systems to detect bot networks [9], fake content [10], or hate speech in social media, among many others, has gained increasing popularity. One may think of fake reviews on Amazon, fake news on user forums, bots on Twitter following/retweeting certain politicians to promote political campaigns, or hate campaigns aimed at systematically attacking certain underprivileged groups with messages full of hate [11, 12]. All of these are growing challenges in online social media networks which demand new machine learning solutions.

Analyzing temporal and contextual patterns in this data is important to discover emerging topics, trends, correlations, causations, and periodic occurrences, happening on real-time data. Data stream mining is the machine learning area devoted to analyzing real-time high-speed online data. This chapter will present some advances on research and applications of data stream mining to problems in online social media.

2. Data stream mining for online learning

A data stream is an ordered and potentially unbounded sequence of data instances arriving continuously to a machine learning system [13]. It is unknown when the volume and speed at which data will arrive to the system. However, it is required to provide a fast prediction, as a delay in the prediction or bottlenecks are not permitted. Moreover, machine learning models need to be continuously updated to make sure they reflect the most up-to-data state of the stream, following

IntechOpen

up with any changes that data may experience with time. Data may evolve with time and experience the appearance or fading of data classes, features, and data distributions. The changes that data may experience with time are known as concept drift [14], and it may be analyzed from multiple perspectives.

Decision boundaries: real vs. virtual drift. Real concept drift has an impact in the classification boundaries, increasing the error when new instances are misclassified. Virtual concept drift observes a change in the distribution of data with time but does not affect the decision boundaries.

Scope of the changes: global vs. local. Global concept drift affects the entire stream, while local affects only certain regions of the feature space or a subset of features.

Speed of drift: incremental vs. gradual. Incremental concept drift is a steady progression from one concept to another. Therefore, it comprises multiple intermediate concepts in between. On the other hand, gradual concept drift reflects a change in a probability distribution in which there is a decreasing probability of observing the old concept and an increasing probability of the new concept to occur.

Concept drift may also suffer from recurrent patterns which happen periodically (e.g., seasonal trends) or blips (noise or random changes that should be ignored and not to be confused with a true drift).

Detecting concept drift is a challenging task itself. There are two types of detectors: explicit and implicit. Explicit concept drift detectors explicitly monitor the characteristics of the stream including statistical distribution variations, density changes, etc. They emit an alert whenever a drift is detected, informing the classifier to update the classification model. Implicit concept drift detectors assume the classifier inherently adapts itself to changes, e.g. by using a dynamic sliding window or by using online learners. How can we detect the emerging of new topics and the fading of others on Twitter? Detecting and anticipating to concept drift remains an open challenge to the machine learning community [15].

Ensemble learning combines multiple classifiers to jointly provide an improved performance compared to single classifiers [16–18]. Ensembles must be composed of mutually complementary and individually competent classifiers, advocating for diversity in its components. Ensembles are natural solvers for stream mining problems with concept drift, as new concepts may be modeled by new components added to the ensemble, whereas older concepts no longer present in the stream may be simply seen their classifiers deleted from the ensemble. Moreover, in the case of recurrent drifts, components may just be disabled (not deleted) so that by the time we anticipate the concept will reoccur, then we may preemptively reenable, avoiding the cost of relearning the classifier, both in terms of lost time and accuracy. One may think about the recommendation systems on Amazon to show the most likely purchased product to users in recurrent seasons (Mother's Day, Christmas, etc.).

Class imbalance is another recurrent problem in data stream mining. Data class distributions may not be evenly represented, plus their proportions may change with time. The majority class may become the minority or reversely. In such a situation, ensembles also help to balance the representativeness of the data and the classification metrics performance as one may want not to bias the algorithms to learn the majority class only. To resolve these issues, several authors have proposed ensembles for drifting, imbalanced streams.

The Kappa Updated Ensemble [16] for drifting data stream mining proposes a hybrid online and batch-based architecture that uses the Kappa statistic for dynamic weighting and selection of classifier components. To achieve ensemble diversity, it proposes to employ different subsets of features on each classifier, along with online bagging. Thanks to the Kappa statistic, it abstains predictions from models that negatively impact the performance of the classifier, increasing the robustness of the ensemble. Abstaining components has also shown to improve the classification in other non-imbalanced streaming problems.

Some real-world problems are characterized for having instances simultaneously categorized into multiple labels. This problem is known as multi-label learning [19–20]. The complexity of correctly classifying the instance increases with the size of the output space. Moreover, concept drift may simultaneously happen to some or many of the labels. Therefore, it is more difficult to detect and adapt to concept drift. Authors have proposed solutions for multi-label data streams, including self-adjusting windows to identify the more accurate and most recent subset of instances in a sliding window [19]. Moreover, punitive systems have shown that penalizing instances leading to erroneous label predictions and early removing them from the window increase the overall accuracy of the classifier [21].

Algorithmic solutions to these open issues in data stream mining come at the expense of an increased computational cost. It would not be possible to provide both an accurate and fast classification and fast update of the classification model if one wants to adapt to concept drift quickly. Therefore, high-performance computing architectures are needed to speed up algorithms in order to meet the real-time constraints of stream learning.

GPUs and MapReduce distributed computing frameworks have become increasingly popular to speed up large-scale data mining problems. They offer higher scalability to big data problems for a fraction of the cost of a traditional mainframe solution. GPUs are particularly efficient for streaming environments and provide a very fast decision with minimum label latency [22–27]. However, they are often associated with a more difficult code implementation and limited memory, which makes it difficult to scale to true big data problems. Distributed GPU solutions may partially alleviate but not solve this problem.

While Apache Hadoop was one of the first and most popular frameworks for MapReduce publicly available, it does not provide the tools nor the speed to work for real-time streams. In such a scenario, there are other solutions much more efficient for real-time streams. Apache Spark Streaming, Apache Flink, and Apache Storm are MapReduce-based frameworks for streaming data [28–32]. However, they lack efficient implementations of effective machine learning algorithms. Therefore, there is a need to implement publicly available methods for stream learning in such frameworks. There are some works on distributed nearest neighbor search and feature selection. However, there is a whole area of asynchronous deep learning models for data streams on MapReduce that is yet to be addressed. While deep learning-based methods may provide the best accuracy, there is also a need to provide interpretable models and demand explanations of the prediction system, particularly for domains requiring accountability, such as medical diagnosis.

3. Conclusions

The popularity of online social media demands new transformative solutions to the emerging problems in social media content and networks, including community detection, bot detection, fake reviews, user behavior prediction, etc. Machine learning provides solutions to these problems, but there are many unresolved open issues. Data stream mining focuses on the analysis of the real-time high-speed streams of data that continuously arrive to a classifier. Data stream mining can detect changes in the property of the stream data and adapt the classification model accordingly. However, there are still too may open issues both from the basic research and application perspectives [32–36] which call for the scientific community to propose new efficient and effective solutions, particularly using high-performance computing architectures.

Acknowledgements

This research was partially supported by the 2018 VCU Presidential Research Quest Fund and an Amazon AWS Machine Learning Research award.

Author details

Alberto Cano
Virginia Commonwealth University, Richmond, VA, USA

*Address all correspondence to: acano@vcu.edu

IntechOpen

© 2020 The Author(s). Licensee IntechOpen. This chapter is distributed under the terms of the Creative Commons Attribution License (http://creativecommons.org/licenses/by/3.0), which permits unrestricted use, distribution, and reproduction in any medium, provided the original work is properly cited. CC BY

References

[1] Stieglitz S, Mirbabaie M, Ross B, Neuberger C. Social media analytics–challenges in topic discovery, data collection, and data preparation. International Journal of Information Management. 2018;**39**:156-168. DOI: 10.1016/j.ijinfomgt.2017.12.002

[2] Batrinca B, Treleaven PC. Social media analytics: A survey of techniques, tools and platforms. AI & Society. 2015;**30**(1):89-116. DOI: 10.1007/s00146-014-0549-4

[3] Emmert-Streib F, Yli-Harja O, Dehmer M. Data analytics applications for streaming data from social media: What to predict? Frontiers in Big Data. 2018;**1**:2. DOI: 10.3389/fdata.2018.00002

[4] Injadat M, Salo F, Nassif AB. Data mining techniques in social media: A survey. Neurocomputing. 2016;**214**:654-670. DOI: 10.1016/j.neucom.2016.06.045

[5] Zatari T. Data mining in social media. International Journal of Scientific and Engineering Research. 2015;**6**(7):152-154

[6] Barbier G, Liu H. Data mining in social media. In: Aggarwal C editor. Social Network Data Analytics. Boston, MA: Springer; 2011:327-352. DOI: 10.1007/978-1-4419-8462-3_12

[7] Feng J, Barbosa LD, Torres V. Systems and methods for social media data mining. United States patent US 9,262,517; 2016

[8] Felt M. Social media and the social sciences: How researchers employ big data analytics. Big Data & Society. 2016;**3**(1):205. DOI: 10.1177/2053951716645828

[9] Flammini A. The rise of social bots. Communications of the ACM. 2016;**59**(7):96-104. DOI: 10.1145/2818717

[10] Shu K, Sliva A, Wang S, Tang J, Liu H. Fake news detection on social media: A data mining perspective. ACM SIGKDD Explorations Newsletter. 2017;**19**(1):22-36. DOI: 10.1145/3137597.3137600

[11] Jain A, Katkar V. Sentiments analysis of twitter data using data mining. In: International Conference on Information Processing. 2015. pp. 807-810

[12] Grossniklaus M, Scholl MH, Weiler A. Towards adaptive event detection techniques for the twitter social media data stream. IEEE Computer Society Technical Committee on Data Engineering. 2015;**38**(4):116-123

[13] Gaber MM, Zaslavsky A, Krishnaswamy S. Mining data streams: A review. ACM Sigmod Record. 2005;**34**(2):18-26. DOI: 10.1145/1083784.1083789

[14] Gama J, Žliobaitė I, Bifet A, Pechenizkiy M, Bouchachia A. A survey on concept drift adaptation. ACM Computing Surveys (CSUR). 2014;**46**(4):44. DOI: 10.1145/2523813

[15] Nguyen DT, Jung JJ. Real-time event detection on social data stream. Mobile Networks and Applications. 2015;**20**(4):475-486. DOI: 10.1007/s11036-014-0557-0

[16] Cano A, Krawczyk B. Kappa updated ensemble for drifting data stream mining. Machine Learning. 2019. DOI: 10.1007/s10994-019-05840-z. (In Press)

[17] Krawczyk B, Cano A. Adaptive ensemble active learning for drifting data stream mining. In: Proceedings of the International Joint Conference on Artificial Intelligence; 10-16 August 2019. Macao; 2019. pp. 2763-2771

[18] Cano A. An ensemble approach to multi-view multi-instance learning. Knowledge-Based Systems. 2017;**136**:46-57. DOI: 10.1016/j.knosys.2017.08.022

[19] Roseberry CA. Multi-label kNN classifier with self adjusting memory for drifting data streams. In: Second International Workshop on Learning with Imbalanced Domains: Theory and Applications, LIDTA@PKDD/ECML; 10-14 September 2018. Dublin; 2018. pp. 23-37

[20] Gonzalez-Lopez J, Ventura S, Cano A. Distributed nearest neighbor classification for large-scale multi-label data on spark. Future Generation Computer Systems. 2018;**87**:66-82. DOI: 10.1016/j.future.2018.04.094

[21] Roseberry M, Krawczyk B, Cano A. Multi-label punitive kNN with self-adjusting memory for drifting data streams. ACM Transactions on Knowledge Discovery from Data. 2019;**13**(6):60. DOI: 10.1145/3363573

[22] Cano A. A survey on graphic processing unit computing for large-scale data mining. Wiley Interdisciplinary Reviews: Data Mining and Knowledge Discovery. 2018;**8**(1):e1232. DOI: 10.1002/widm.1232

[23] Cano A, Krawczyk B. Evolving rule-based classifiers with genetic programming on GPUs for drifting data streams. Pattern Recognition. 2019;**87**:248-268. DOI: 10.1016/j.patcog.2018.10.024

[24] Cano A, Krawczyk B. Learning classification rules with differential evolution for high-speed data stream mining on GPUs. In: Proceedings of the IEEE Congress on Evolutionary Computation; 8-13 July 2018. Rio de Janeiro, New York: IEEE; 2018. pp. 197-204

[25] Cano A, Zafra A, Ventura S. Parallel evaluation of Pittsburgh rule-based classifiers on GPUs. Neurocomputing. 2014;**126**:45-57. DOI: 10.1016/j.neucom.2013.01.049

[26] Cano A, Ventura S, Cios K. Scalable CAIM discretization on multiple GPUs using concurrent kernels. The Journal of Supercomputing. 2014;**69**(1):273-292. DOI: 10.1007/s11227-014-1151-8

[27] Cano A, Zafra A, Ventura S. Solving classification problems using genetic programming algorithms on GPUs. In: 5th International Conference on Hybrid Artificial Intelligent Systems (HAIS); 23-25 May 2010. Wroclaw; 2010. pp. 17-26

[28] Cano A, Garcia C, Ventura S. Extremely high-dimensional optimization with MapReduce: Scaling functions and algorithm. Information Sciences. 2017;**415-416**:110-127. DOI: 10.1016/j.ins.2017.06.024

[29] Gonzalez-Lopez J, Ventura S, Cano A. Distributed selection of continuous features in multi-label classification using mutual information. IEEE Transactions on Neural Networks and Learning Systems. 2019. DOI: 10.1109/TNNLS.2019.2944298. (In Press)

[30] Gonzalez-Lopez J, Ventura S, Cano A. Distributed multi-label feature selection using individual mutual information measures. Knowledge-Based Systems. 2019. DOI: 10.1016/j.knosys.2019.105052. (In Press)

[31] Krawczyk B, Cano A. Online ensemble learning with abstaining classifiers for drifting and noisy data streams. Applied Soft Computing. 2018;**68**:677-692

[32] Korycki, Cano A, Krawczyk B. Active learning with abstaining classifiers for imbalanced drifting data streams. In: Proceedings of the IEEE International Conference on BigData; 9-12 December. Los Angeles, New York: IEEE; 2019. p. 2019

[33] Wu Y, Cao N, Gotz D, Tan YP, Keim DA. A survey on visual analytics of social media data. IEEE Transactions on Multimedia. 2016;**18**(11):2135-2148. DOI: 10.1109/TMM.2016.2614220

[34] Grimmer J. We are all social scientists now: How big data, machine learning, and causal inference work together. Political Science & Politics. 2015;**48**(1):80-83. DOI: 10.1017/S1049096514001784

[35] Tsou M. Research challenges and opportunities in mapping social media and big data. Cartography and Geographic Information Science. 2015;**42**(sup 1):70-74. DOI: 10.1080/15230406.2015.1059251

[36] Bello-Orgaz G, Jung JJ, Camacho D. Social big data: Recent achievements and new challenges. Information Fusion. 2016;**28**:45-59. DOI: 10.1016/j.inffus.2015.08.005

Chapter 2

Automatic Speech Emotion Recognition Using Machine Learning

Leila Kerkeni, Youssef Serrestou, Mohamed Mbarki, Kosai Raoof, Mohamed Ali Mahjoub and Catherine Cleder

Abstract

This chapter presents a comparative study of speech emotion recognition (SER) systems. Theoretical definition, categorization of affective state and the modalities of emotion expression are presented. To achieve this study, an SER system, based on different classifiers and different methods for features extraction, is developed. Mel-frequency cepstrum coefficients (MFCC) and modulation spectral (MS) features are extracted from the speech signals and used to train different classifiers. Feature selection (FS) was applied in order to seek for the most relevant feature subset. Several machine learning paradigms were used for the emotion classification task. A recurrent neural network (RNN) classifier is used first to classify seven emotions. Their performances are compared later to multivariate linear regression (MLR) and support vector machines (SVM) techniques, which are widely used in the field of emotion recognition for spoken audio signals. Berlin and Spanish databases are used as the experimental data set. This study shows that for Berlin database all classifiers achieve an accuracy of 83% when a speaker normalization (SN) and a feature selection are applied to the features. For Spanish database, the best accuracy (94 %) is achieved by RNN classifier without SN and with FS.

Keywords: speech emotion recognition, feature extraction recurrent neural, network SVM, multivariate linear regression, MFCC, modulation spectral features, machine learning

1. Introduction

Emotion plays a significant role in daily interpersonal human interactions. This is essential to our rational as well as intelligent decisions. It helps us to match and understand the feelings of others by conveying our feelings and giving feedback to others. Research has revealed the powerful role that emotion play in shaping human social interaction. Emotional displays convey considerable information about the mental state of an individual. This has opened up a new research field called automatic emotion recognition, having basic goals to understand and retrieve desired emotions. In prior studies, several modalities have been explored to recognize the emotional states such as facial expressions [1], speech [2], physiological signals [3], etc. Several inherent advantages make speech signals a good source for affective computing. For example, compared to many other biological signals (e.g., electrocardiogram), speech signals usually can be acquired more readily and economically. This is why the majority of researchers are interested in speech emotion recognition (SER). SER aims to recognize the underlying emotional state of a speaker from her voice. The area has received increasing research interest all through current years. There are many applications of detecting the emotion of the persons like in the interface with robots, audio surveillance, web-based E-learning, commercial applications, clinical studies, entertainment, banking, call centers, cardboard systems, computer games, etc. For classroom orchestration or E-learning, information about the emotional state of students can provide focus on the enhancement of teaching quality. For example, a teacher can use SER to decide what subjects can be taught and must be able to develop strategies for managing emotions within the learning environment. That is why learner's emotional state should be considered in the classroom.

Three key issues need to be addressed for successful SER system, namely, (1) choice of a good emotional speech database, (2) extracting effective features, and (3) designing reliable classifiers using machine learning algorithms. In fact, the emotional feature extraction is a main issue in the SER system. Many researchers [4] have proposed important speech features which contain emotion information, such as energy, pitch, formant frequency, Linear Prediction Cepstrum Coefficients (LPCC), Mel-frequency cepstrum coefficients (MFCC), and modulation spectral features (MSFs) [5]. Thus, most researchers prefer to use combining feature set that is composed of many kinds of features containing more emotional information [6]. However, using a combining feature set may give rise to high dimension and redundancy of speech features; thereby, it makes the learning process complicated for most machine learning algorithms and increases the likelihood of overfitting. Therefore, feature selection is indispensable to reduce the dimensions redundancy of features. A review for feature selection models and techniques is presented in [7]. Both feature extraction and feature selection are capable of improving learning performance, lowering computational complexity, building better generalizable models, and decreasing required storage. The last step of speech emotion recognition is classification. It involves classifying the raw data in the form of utterance or frame of the utterance into a particular class of emotion on the basis of features extracted from the data. In recent years in speech emotion recognition, researchers proposed many classification algorithms, such as Gaussian mixture model (GMM) [8], hidden Markov model (HMM) [9], support vector machine (SVM) [10–14], neural networks (NN) [15], and recurrent neural networks (RNN) [16–18]. Some other types of classifiers are also proposed by some researchers such as a modified brain emotional learning model (BEL) [19] in which the adaptive neuro-fuzzy inference system (ANFIS) and multilayer perceptron (MLP) are merged for speech emotion recognition. Another proposed strategy is a multiple kernel Gaussian process (GP) classification [17], in which two similar notions in the learning algorithm are presented by combining the linear kernel and radial basis function (RBF) kernel. The Voiced Segment Selection (VSS) algorithm also proposed in [20] deals with the voiced signal segment as the texture image processing feature which is different from the traditional method. It uses the Log-Gabor filters to extract the voiced and unvoiced features from spectrogram to make the classification.

In previous work [21], we present a system for the recognition of «seven acted emotional states (anger, disgust, fear, joy, sadness, and surprise)». To do that, we extracted the MFCC and MS features and used them to train three different machine learning paradigms (MLR, SVM, and RNN). We demonstrated that the combination of both features has a high accuracy above 94% on the Spanish database. All previously published works generally use the Berlin database. To our knowledge, the Spanish emotional database has never been used before. For this reason, we have chosen to compare them. In this chapter, we concentrate to improve accuracy; more experiments have been performed. This chapter mainly makes the following contributions:

- The effect of speaker normalization (SN) is also studied, which removes the mean of features and normalizes them to unit variance. Experiments are performed under a speaker-independent condition.

- Additionally, a feature selection technique is assessed to obtain good features from the set of features extracted in [21].

The rest of the chapter is organized as follows. In the next section, we start by introducing the nature of speech emotions. Section 3 describes features we extracted from a speech signal. A feature selection method and machine learning algorithms used for SER are presented. Section 4 reports on the databases we used and presents the simulation results obtained using different features and different machine learning (ML) paradigms. Section 5 closes this chapter by analyses and conclusion.

2. Emotion and classification

This section is concerned with defining the term emotion, presenting its different models. Also for recognizing emotions, there are several techniques and inputs that can be used. A brief description of all of the techniques is presented here.

2.1 Definition

A definition is both important and difficult because the everyday word "emotion" is a notoriously fluid term in meaning. Emotion is one of the most difficult concepts to define in psychology. In fact, there are different definitions of emotions in the scientific literature. In everyday speech, emotion is any relatively brief conscious experience characterized by intense mental activity and a high degree of pleasure or displeasure [22, 23]. Scientific discourse has drifted to other meanings and there is no consensus on a definition. Emotion is often entwined with temperament, mood, personality, motivation, and disposition. In psychology, emotion is frequently defined as a complex state of feeling that results in physical and psychological changes. These changes influence thought and behavior. According to other theories, emotions are not causal forces but simply syndromes of components such as motivation, feeling, behavior, and physiological changes [24]. In 1884, in *What is an emotion?* [25], American psychologist and philosopher William James proposed a theory of emotion whose influence was considerable. According to his thesis, the feeling of intense emotion corresponds to the perception of specific bodily changes. This approach is found in many current theories: the bodily reaction is the cause and not the consequence of the emotion. The scope of this theory is measured by the many debates it provokes. This illustrates the difficulty of agreeing on a definition of this dynamic and complex phenomenon that we call emotion. "Emotion" refers to a wide range of affective processes such as moods, feelings, affects, and well-being [26]. The term "emotion" in [6] has been also referred to an extremely complex state associated with a wide variety of mental, physiological, and physical events.

2.2 Categorization of emotions

The categorization of emotions has long been a hot subject of debate in different fields of psychology, affective science, and emotion research. It is mainly based on two popular approaches: categorical (termed discrete) and dimensional (termed continuous). In the first approach, emotions are described with a discrete number of classes. Many theorists have conducted studies to determine which emotions are basic [27]. A most popular example is Ekman [28] who proposed a list of six basic emotions, which are anger, disgust, fear, happiness, sadness, and surprise. He explains that each emotion acts as a discrete category rather than an individual emotional state. In the second approach, emotions are a combination of several psychological dimensions and identified by axes. Other researchers define emotions according to one or more dimensions. Wilhelm Max Wundt proposed in 1897 that emotions can be described by three dimensions: (1) strain versus relaxation, (2) pleasurable versus unpleasurable, and (3) arousing versus subduing [29]. PAD emotional state model is another three-dimensional approach by Albert Mehrabian and James Russell where PAD stands for pleasure, arousal, and dominance. Another popular dimensional model was proposed by James Russell in 1977. Unlike the earlier three-dimensional models, Russell's model features only two dimensions which include (1) arousal (or activation) and (2) valence (or evaluation) [29].

The categorical approach is commonly used in SER [30]. It characterizes emotions used in everyday emotion words such as joy and anger. In this work, a set of six basic emotions (anger, disgust, fear, joy, sadness, and surprise) plus neutral, corresponding to the six emotions of Ekman's model, were used for the recognition of emotion from speech using the categorical approach.

2.3 Sensory modalities for emotion expression

There is vigorous debate about what exactly individual can express nonverbally. Humans can express their emotions through many different types of nonverbal communication including facial expressions, quality of speech produced, and physiological signals of the human body. In this section, we discuss each of these categories.

2.3.1 Facial expressions

The human face is extremely expressive, able to express countless emotions without saying a word [31]. And unlike some forms of nonverbal communication, facial expressions are universal. The facial expressions for happiness, sadness, anger, surprise, fear, and disgust are the same across cultures.

2.3.2 Speech

In addition to faces, voices are an important modality for emotional expression. Speech is a relevant communicational channel enriched with emotions: the voice in speech not only conveys a semantic message but also the information about the emotional state of the speaker. Some important voice feature vectors that have been chosen for research such as fundamental frequency, mel-frequency cepstral coefficient (MFCC), prediction cepstral coefficient (LPCC), etc.

2.3.3 Physiological signals

The physiological signals related to autonomic nervous system allow to assess objectively emotions. These include electroencephalogram (EEG), heart rate (HR), electrocardiogram (ECG), respiration (RSP), blood pressure (BP), electromyogram (EMG), skin conductance (SC), blood volume pulse (BVP), and skin temperature (ST) [32]. Using physiological signals to recognize emotions is also helpful to those people who suffer from physical or mental illness thus exhibit problems with facial expressions or tone of voice.

3. Speech emotion recognition (SER) system

3.1 Block diagram

Our SER system consists of four main steps. First is the voice sample collection. The second features vector that is formed by extracting the features. As the next step, we tried to determine which features are most relevant to differentiate each emotion. These features are introduced to machine learning classifier for recognition. This process is described in **Figure 1**.

3.2. Feature extraction

The speech signal contains a large number of parameters that reflect the emotional characteristics. One of the sticking points in emotion recognition is what features should be used. In recent research, many common features are extracted, such as energy, pitch, formant, and some spectrum features such as linear prediction coefficients (LPC), mel-frequency cepstrum coefficients (MFCC), and modulation spectral features. In this work, we have selected modulation spectral features and MFCC, to extract the emotional features.

Mel-frequency cepstrum coefficient (MFCC) is the most used representation of the spectral property of voice signals. These are the best for speech recognition as it takes human perception sensitivity with respect to frequencies into consideration. For each frame, the Fourier transform and the energy spectrum were estimated and mapped into the Mel-frequency scale. The discrete cosine transform (DCT) of the Mel log energies was estimated, and the first 12 DCT coefficients provided the

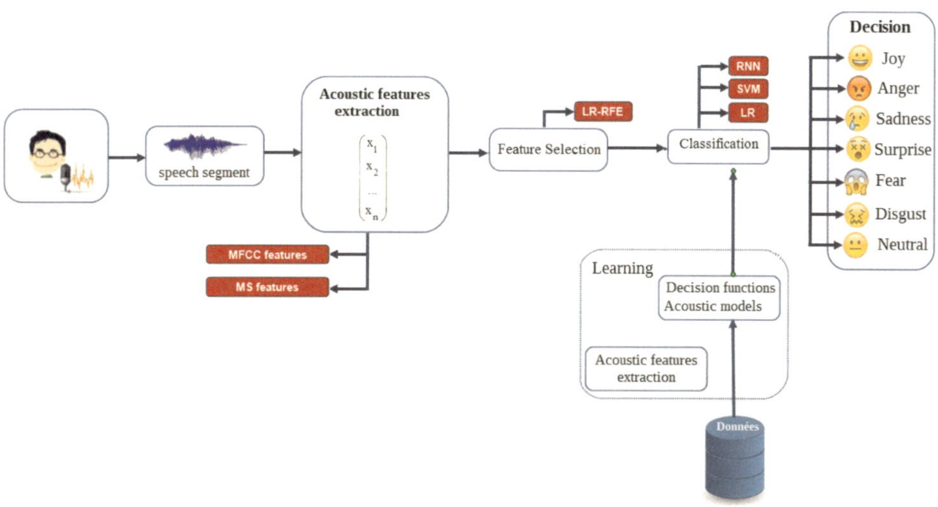

Figure 1.
Block diagram of the proposed system.

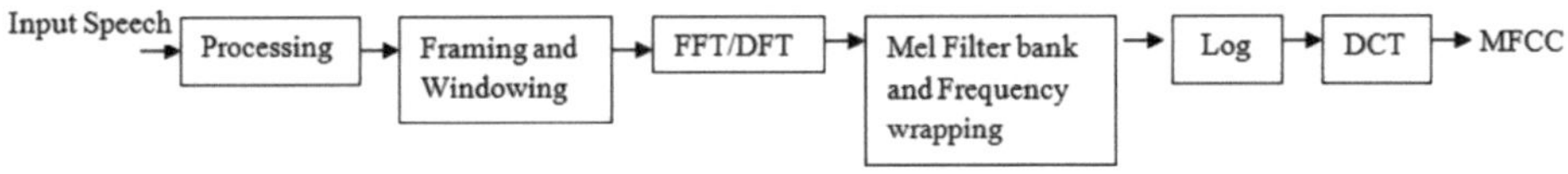

Figure 2.
Schema of MFCC extraction [33].

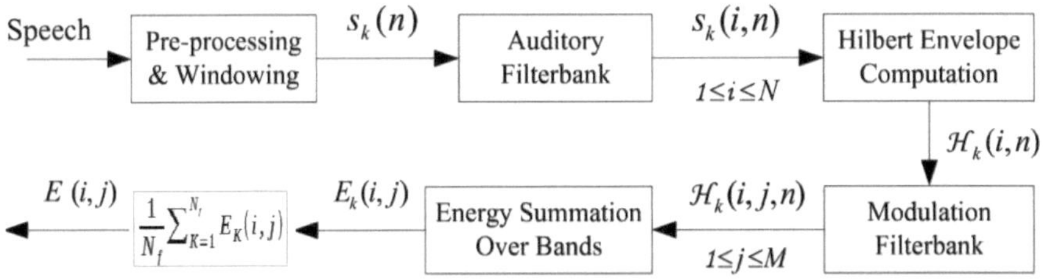

Figure 3.
Process for computing the ST representation [5].

MFCC values used in the classification process. Usually, the process of calculating MFCC is shown in **Figure 2**.

In our research, we extract the first 12 order of the MFCC coefficients where the speech signals are sampled at 16 KHz. For each order coefficients, we calculate the mean, variance, standard deviation, kurtosis, and skewness, and this is for the other all the frames of an utterance. Each MFCC feature vector is 60-dimensional.

Modulation spectral features (MSFs) are extracted from an auditory-inspired long-term spectro-temporal representation. These features are obtained by emulating the spectro-temporal (ST) processing performed in the human auditory system and consider regular acoustic frequency jointly with modulation frequency. The steps for computing the ST representation are illustrated in **Figure 3**. In order to obtain the ST representation, the speech signal is first decomposed by an auditory filterbank (19 filters in total). The Hilbert envelopes of the critical-band outputs are computed to form the modulation signals. A modulation filterbank is further applied to the Hilbert envelopes to perform frequency analysis. The spectral contents of the modulation signals are referred to as modulation spectra, and the proposed features are thereby named modulation spectral features (MSFs) [5]. Lastly, the ST representation is formed by measuring the energy of the decomposed envelope signals, as a function of regular acoustic frequency and modulation frequency. The energy, taken over all frames in every spectral band, provides a feature. In our experiment, an auditory filterbank with $N = 19$ filters and a modulation filterbank with $M = 5$ filters are used. In total, 95 (19×5) MSFs are calculated in this work from the ST representation.

3.3 Feature selection

As reported by Aha and Bankert [34], the objective of feature selection in ML is to "reduce the number of features used to characterize a dataset so as to improve a learning algorithm's performance on a given task." The objective will be the maximization of the classification accuracy in a specific task for a certain learning algorithm; as a collateral effect, the number of features to induce the final classification model will be reduced. Feature selection (FS) aims to choose a subset of the relevant features from the original ones according to certain relevance evaluation criterion, which usually leads to higher recognition accuracy [35]. It can drastically reduce the running time of the learning algorithms. In this section, we present an effective feature selection method used in our work, named recursive feature elimination with linear regression (LR-RFE).

Recursive feature elimination (RFE) uses a model (e.g., linear regression or SVM) to select either the best- or worst-performing feature and then excludes this feature. These estimators assign weights to features (e.g., the coefficients of a linear model), so the goal of recursive feature elimination (RFE) is to select features by recursively considering smaller and smaller sets of features. First, the estimator is trained on the initial set of features, and the predictive power of each feature is measured [36]. Then, the least important features are removed from the current set of features. That procedure is recursively repeated on the pruned set until the desired number of features to select is eventually reached. In this work, we implemented the recursive feature elimination method of feature ranking via the use of basic linear regression (LR-RFE) [37]. Other research also uses RFE with another linear model such as SVM-RFE that is an SVM-based feature selection algorithm created by [38]. Using SVM-RFE, Guyon et al. selected key and important feature sets. In addition to improving the classification accuracy rate, it can reduce classification computational time.

3.4 Classification methods

Many machine learning algorithms have been used for discrete emotion classification. The goal of these algorithms is to learn from the training samples and then use this learning to classify new observation. In fact, there is no definitive answer to the choice of the learning algorithm; every technique has its own advantages and limitations. For this reason, here we chose to compare the performance of three different classifiers.

Multivariate linear regression classification (MLR) is a simple and efficient computation of machine learning algorithms, and it can be used for both regression and classification problems. We have slightly modified the LRC algorithm described as follow Algorithm 1 [39]. We calculated (in step 3) the absolute value of the difference between original and predicted response vectors ($|y - y_i|$), instead of the Euclidean distance between them ($\|y - y_i\|$).

Support vector machines (SVM) are an optimal margin classifier in machine learning. It is also used extensively in many studies that related to audio emotion recognition which can be found in [10, 13, 14]. It can have a very good classification performance compared to other classifiers especially for limited training data [11]. SVM theoretical background can be found in [40]. A MATLAB toolbox implementing SVM is freely available in [41]. A polynomial kernel is investigated in this work.

Algorithm 1. Linear Regression Classification (LRC)

Inputs: Class models $X_i \in \mathbb{R}^{q \times p_i}$, $i = 1, 2, \ldots, N$ and a test speech vector $y \in \mathbb{R}^{q \times 1}$
Output: Class of y

1. $\hat{\beta}_i \in \mathbb{R}^{p_i \times 1}$ is evaluated against each class model, $\hat{\beta}_i = \left(X_i^T X_i\right)^{(-1)} X_i^T y$, $i = 1, 2, \ldots, N$
2. $\hat{y}_i$ is computed for each $\hat{\beta}_i$, $\hat{y}_i = X_i \hat{\beta}_i$, $\quad i = 1, 2, \ldots, N$;
3. Distance calculation between original and predicted response variables $d_i(y) = |y - y_i|$, $\quad i = 1, 2, \ldots, N$;
4. Decision is made in favor of the class with the minimum distance $d_i(y)$

Recurrent neural networks (RNN) are suitable for learning time series data, and it has shown improved performance for classification task [42]. While RNN

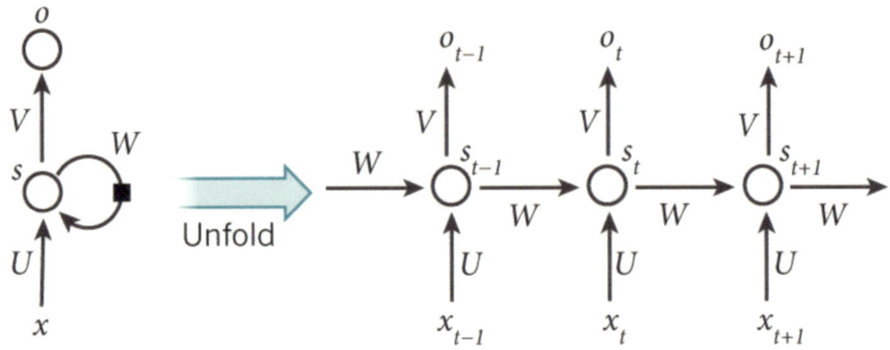

Figure 4.
A basic concept of RNN and unfolding in time of the computation involved in its forward computation [18].

models are effective at learning temporal correlations, they suffer from the vanishing gradient problem which increases with the length of the training sequences. To resolve this problem, long short-term memory (LSTM) RNNs were proposed by Hochreiter et al. [43]; it uses memory cells to store information so that it can exploit long-range dependencies in the data [17].

Figure 4 shows a basic concept of RNN implementation. Unlike traditional neural network that uses different parameters at each layer, the RNN shares the same parameters (U, V, and W are presented in **Figure 4**) across all steps. The hidden state formulas and variables are as follows:

$$s_t = f(Ux_t + Ws_{t-1})$$

where x_t, s_t, and o_t are respectively the input, the hidden state, and the output at time step t and U, V, W are parameters matrices.

4. Experimental results and analysis

4.1 Emotional speech databases

The performance and robustness of the recognition systems will be easily affected if it is not well trained with a suitable database. Therefore, it is essential to have sufficient and suitable phrases in the database to train the emotion recognition system and subsequently evaluate its performance. There are three main types of databases: acted emotions, natural spontaneous emotions, and elicited emotions [27, 44]. In this work, we used an acted emotion databases because they contain strong emotional expressions. The literature on speech emotion recognition [45] shows that the majority of studies have been conducted with emotional acted speech. In this section, we detailed the two emotional speech databases used for classifying discrete emotions in our experiments: Berlin Database and Spanish Database.

4.2 Berlin database

The Berlin database [46] is widely used in emotional speech recognition. It contains 535 utterances spoken by 10 actors (5 female, 5 male) in 7 simulated emotions (anger, boredom, disgust, fear, joy, sadness, and neutral). This database was chosen for the following reasons: (i) the quality of its recording is very good, and (ii) it is public [47] and popular database of emotion recognition that is recommended in the literature [19].

4.3 Spanish database

The INTER1SP Spanish emotional database contains utterances from two professional actors (one female and one male speaker).The Spanish corpus that we have the right to access (free for academic and research use) [48] was recorded twice in the «six basic emotions plus neutral (anger, sadness, joy, fear, disgust, surprise and neutral/normal)». Four additional neutral variations (soft, loud, slow, and fast) were recorded once. This is preferred to other created database because it is available for researchers use and it contains more data (6041 utterances in total). This paper has focused on only seven main emotions from the Spanish database in order to achieve a higher and more accurate rate of recognition and to make the comparison with the Berlin database detailed above.

4.4 Results and analysis

In this section, experimentation results are presented and discussed. We report the recognition accuracy of using MLR, SVM, and RNN classifiers. Experimental evaluation is performed on the Berlin and Spanish databases. All classification results are obtained under tenfold cross-validation. Cross-validation is a common practice used in performance analysis that randomly partitions the data into N complementary subsets, with $N - 1$ of them used for training in each validation and the remaining one used for testing. The neural network structure used is a simple LSTM. It consists of two consecutive LSTM layers with hyperbolic tangent activation followed by two classification dense layers. Features from data are scaled to $[-1, 1]$ before applying classifiers. Scaling features before recognition is important, because when a learning phase is fit on unscaled data, it is possible for large inputs to slow down the learning and convergence and in some cases prevent the used classifier from effectively learning for the classification problem. The effect of speaker normalization (SN) step prior to recognition is investigated, and there are three different SN schemes that are defined in [6]. SN is useful to compensate for the variations due to speaker diversity rather than the change of emotional state. We used in this section the SN scheme that has given the best results in [6]. The features of each speaker are normalized with a mean of 0 and a standard deviation of 1. **Tables 1–3** show the recognition rate for each combination of various features and classifiers based on Berlin and Spanish databases. These experiments use feature set without feature selection. As shown in **Table 1**, SVM classifier yields better results above 81%, with feature combination of MFCC and MS for Berlin database. Our results have improved compared to previous results in [21] because we changed the SVM parameters for each type of features to develop a good model.

From **Table 1**, it can be concluded that applying SN improves recognition results for Berlin database. But this is not the case for the Spanish database, as demonstrated in **Tables 2** and **3**. Results are the same with the three different classifiers. This can be explained by the number of speakers in each database. The Berlin database contains 10 different speakers, compared to the Spanish database that contains only two speakers and probably the language impact. As regarding the RNN method, we found that combining both types of features has the worst recognition rate for the Berlin database, as shown in **Table 3**. That is because the RNN model has too many parameters (155 coefficients in total) and a poor training data. This is the phenomena of overfitting. This is confirmed by the fact that when we reduced the number of features from 155 to 59 features, the results show an increase of above 13%, as shown in **Table 4**. To investigate whether a smaller feature space leads to better recognition performance, we repeated all evaluations on the development set by applying a recursive feature elimination (LR-RFE) for each modality

				Recognition rate (%)								
Test	Feature	Method	SN	A	E	F	L	N	T	W	AVG.	(σ)
#1	MS	MLR	No	45.90	45.72	48.78	77.08	59.43	79.91	75.94	66.23	(5.85)
	MFCC			56.55	62.28	45.60	54.97	57.35	74.36	91.37	64.70	(3.20)
	MFCC+SM			70.26	73.04	51.95	82.44	69.55	82.49	76.55	73.00	(3.23)
#2	MS	SVM	No	56.61	54.78	51.17	70.98	67.32	67.50	73.13	70.63	(6.45)
	MFCC			73.99	64.14	64.76	55.30	62.28	84.13	83.13	71.70	(4.24)
	MFCC+SM			82.03	68.70	69.09	79.16	76.99	80.89	80.63	81.10	(2.73)
#3	MS	MLR	Yes	48.98	35.54	32.66	80.35	55.54	88.79	85.77	64.20	(5.27)
	MFCC			59.71	59.72	48.65	67.10	67.98	91.73	87.51	71.00	(4.19)
	MFCC+SM			72.32	68.82	51.98	82.60	81.72	91.96	80.71	75.25	(2.49)
#4	MS	SVM	Yes	62.72	49.44	37.29	76.14	71.30	88.44	80.15	71.90	(2.38)
	MFCC			70.68	56.55	56.99	59.88	68.14	91.88	85.44	77.60	(4.35)
	MFCC+SM			77.37	69.67	58.16	79.87	88.57	98.75	86.64	81.00	(2.45)

Berlin (a, fear; e, disgust; f, happiness; l, boredom; n, neutral; t, sadness; w, anger).

Table 1.
Recognition results with MS, MFCC features, and their combination on Berlin database; AVG. denotes average recognition rate; σ denotes standard deviation of the 10-cross-validation accuracies.

				Recognition rate (%)								
Test	Feature	Method	SN	A	D	F	J	N	S	T	AVG.	(σ)
#1	MS	MLR	No	67.72	44.04	68.78	46.95	89.58	63.10	78.49	69.22	(1.37)
	MFCC			67.85	61.41	75.97	60.17	95.79	71.89	84.94	77.21	(0.76)
	MFCC+SM			78.75	78.18	80.68	63.84	96.80	82.44	89.01	83.55	(0.55)
#2	MS	SVM	No	70.33	69.38	78.09	60.97	89.25	69.38	85.95	80.98	(1.09)
	MFCC			79.93	79.02	81.81	75.71	93.77	80.15	92.01	90.94	(0.93)
	MFCC+SM			84.90	88.26	89.44	80.90	96.58	83.89	95.63	89.69	(0.62)
#3	MS	MLR	Yes	64.76	49.02	66.87	44.52	87.50	58.26	78.70	67.84	(1.27)
	MFCC			66.54	57.83	74.56	56.98	94.02	72.32	89.63	76.47	(1.51)
	MFCC+SM			77.01	78.45	80.50	64.18	94.42	80.14	91.29	83.03	(0.97)
#4	MS	SVM	Yes	69.81	70.35	75.44	52.60	86.77	66.94	82.57	78.40	(1.64)
	MFCC			77.45	77.41	80.99	69.47	91.89	75.17	93.50	87.47	(0.95)
	MFCC+SM			85.28	84.54	84.49	73.47	93.43	81.79	94.04	86.57	(0.72)

Spanish (a, anger; d, disgust; f, fear; j, joy; n, neutral; s, surprise; t, sadness).

Table 2.
Recognition results with MS, MFCC features, and their combination on Spanish database.

combination. The stability of RFE depends heavily on the type of model that is used for feature ranking at each iteration. In our case, we tested the RFE based on an SVM and regression models; we found that using linear regression provides more stable results. We observed from the previous results that the combination of the features gives the best results. So we applied LR-RFE feature selection only for this combination to improve accuracy. In this work, a total of 155 features were used;

Dataset	Feature	SN	Average (avg)	Standard deviation (σ)
Berlin	MS	No	66.32	5.93
	MFCC		69.55	3.91
	MFCC+MS	Yes	63.67	7.74
	MS		68.94	5.65
	MFCC		73.08	5.17
	MFCC+MS		76.98	4.79
Spanish	MS	No	82.30	2.88
	MFCC		86.56	2.80
	MFCC+MS		90.05	1.64
	MS	Yes	82.14	1.67
	MFCC		86.21	1.22
	MFCC+MS		87.02	0.36

Table 3.
Recognition results using RNN classifier based on Berlin and Spanish databases.

best features were chosen from feature selection. Fifty-nine features were selected by RFE feature selection method based on LR from the Berlin database and 110 features from the Spanish database. The corresponding results of LR-RFE can be seen in **Table 4**. For most setting using the Spanish database, LR-RFE does not significantly improve the average accuracy. However, for recognition based on Berlin database using the three classifiers, LR-RFE leads to a remarkable performance gain, as shown in **Figure 5**. This increases the average of MFCC combined with MS features from 63.67 to 78.11% for RNN classifier. These results are illustrated in **Table 4**. For the Spanish database, the feature combination of MFCC and MS after applying LR-RFE selection using RNN has the best recognition rate which is above 94.01%.

SN	Classifier	LR-RFE	Berlin	Spanish
No	MLR	No	73.00 (3.23)	83.55 (0.55)
		Yes	79.40 (3.09)	84.19 (0.96)
	SVM	No	81.10 (2.73)	89.69 (0.62)
		Yes	80.90 (3.17)	90.05 (0.80)
	RNN	No	63.67 (7.74)	90.05 (1.64)
		Yes	78.11 (3.53)	**94.01** (0.76)
Yes	MLR	No	75.25 (2.49)	83.03 (0.97)
		Yes	**83.20** (3.25)	82.27 (1.12)
	SVM	No	81.00 (2.45)	86.57 (0.72)
		Yes	**83.90** (2.46)	86.47 (1.34)
	RNN	No	76.98 (4.79)	87.02 (0.36)
		Yes	**83.42** (0.70)	85.00 (0.93)

Table 4.
Recognition results with combination of MFCC and MS features using ML paradigm before and after applying LR-RFE feature selection method (Berlin and Spanish databases).

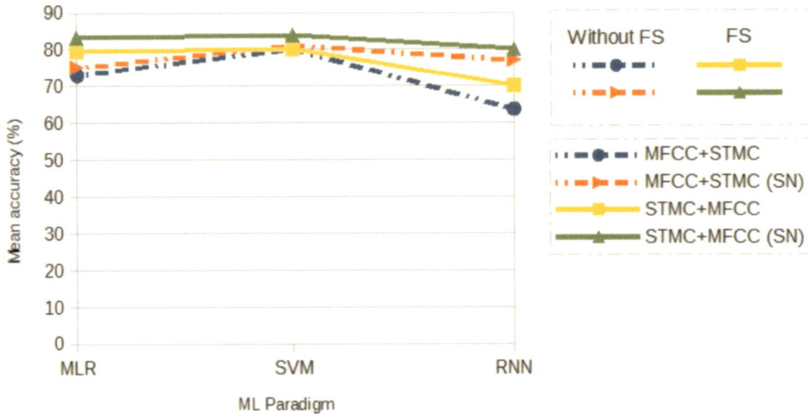

Figure 5.
Performance comparison of three machine learning paradigms (MLR, SVM, RNN) using speaker normalization (SN) and RFE feature selection (FS), for the Berlin database, is shown.

Emotion	Anger	Disgust	Fear	Joy	Neutral	Surprise	Sadness	Rate (%)
Anger	79	1	0	1	2	3	0	91.86
Disgust	0	67	3	0	1	0	1	93.05
Fear	0	3	70	0	1	0	2	93.33
Joy	3	1	1	71	0	0	0	93.42
Neutral	2	0	1	0	156	0	1	97.50
surprise	2	1	0	3	0	60	0	92.30
Sadness	0	0	1	0	2	0	66	95.65
Precision (%)	91.86	91.78	92.10	94.66	96.29	95.23	94.28	

Table 5.
Confusion matrix for feature combination after LR-RFE selection based on Spanish database.

The confusion matrix for the best recognition of emotions using MFCC and MS features with RNN based on Spanish database is shown in **Table 5**. The rate column lists per class recognition rates and precision for a class are the number of samples correctly classified divided by the total number of samples classified to the class. It can be seen that *Neutral* was the emotion that was least difficult to recognize from speech as opposed to *Disgust* which was the most difficult and it forms the most notable confusion pair with *Fear*.

5. Conclusion

In this current study, we presented an automatic speech emotion recognition (SER) system using three machine learning algorithms (MLR, SVM, and RNN) to classify seven emotions. Thus, two types of features (MFCC and MS) were extracted from two different acted databases (Berlin and Spanish databases), and a combination of these features was presented. In fact, we study how classifiers and features impact recognition accuracy of emotions in speech. A subset of highly discriminant features is selected. Feature selection techniques show that more information is not always good in machine learning applications. The machine learning models were trained and evaluated to recognize emotional states from these features. SER reported the best recognition rate of 94% on the Spanish database using RNN classifier without speaker normalization (SN) and with feature selection (FS). For Berlin database, all of the classifiers achieve an accuracy of 83% when a speaker normalization (SN) and a feature selection (FS) are applied to the features. From this result, we can see that RNN often perform better with more data and it suffers from the problem of very long training times. Therefore, we concluded that the SVM and MLR models have a good potential for practical usage for limited data in comparison with RNN .

Enhancement of the robustness of emotion recognition system is still possible by combining databases and by fusion of classifiers. The effect of training multiple emotion detectors can be investigated by fusing these into a single detection system. We aim also to use other feature selection methods because the quality of the feature selection affects the emotion recognition rate: a good emotion feature selection method can select features reflecting emotion state quickly. The overall aim of our work is to develop a system that will be used in a pedagogical interaction in classrooms, in order to help the teacher to orchestrate his class. For achieving this goal, we aim to test the system proposed in this work.

Author details

Leila Kerkeni[1,2]*, Youssef Serrestou[1], Mohamed Mbarki[3], Kosai Raoof[1], Mohamed Ali Mahjoub[2] and Catherine Cleder[4]

1 LAUM UMR CNRS 6613, Le Mans Université, France

2 LATIS Lab, ENISo Université de Sousse, Tunisia

3 ISSAT, Université de Sousse, Tunisia

4 CREN Lab, Université de Nantes, France

*Address all correspondence to: kerkeni.leila@gmail.com

IntechOpen

© 2019 The Author(s). Licensee IntechOpen. This chapter is distributed under the terms of the Creative Commons Attribution License (http://creativecommons.org/licenses/by/3.0), which permits unrestricted use, distribution, and reproduction in any medium, provided the original work is properly cited.

References

[1] Ali H, Hariharan M, Yaacob S, Adom AH. Facial emotion recognition using empirical mode decomposition. Expert Systems with Applications. 2015;**42**(3): 1261-1277

[2] Liu ZT, Wu M, Cao WH, Mao JW, Xu JP, Tan GZ. Speech emotion recognition based on feature selection and extreme learning machine decision tree. Neurocomputing. 2018;**273**: 271-280

[3] Ragot M, Martin N, Em S, Pallamin N, Diverrez JM. Emotion recognition using physiological signals: Laboratory vs. wearable sensors. In: International Conference on Applied Human Factors and Ergonomics. Springer; 2017. pp. 15-22

[4] Surabhi V, Saurabh M. Speech emotion recognition: A review. International Research Journal of Engineering and Technology (IRJET). 2016;**03**:313-316

[5] Wu S, Falk TH, Chan WY. Automatic speech emotion recognition using modulation spectral features. Speech Communication. 2011;**53**:768-785

[6] Wu S. Recognition of human emotion in speech using modulation spectral features and support vector machines [PhD thesis]. 2009

[7] Tang J, Alelyani S, Liu H. Feature selection for classification: A review. Data Classification: Algorithms and Applications. 2014:37

[8] Martin V, Robert V. Recognition of emotions in German speech using Gaussian mixture models. LNAI. 2009; **5398**:256-263

[9] Ingale AB, Chaudhari D. Speech emotion recognition using hidden Markov model and support vector machine. International Journal of Advanced Engineering Research and Studies. 2012:316-318

[10] Milton A, Sharmy Roy S, Tamil Selvi S. SVM scheme for speech emotion recognition using MFCC feature. International Journal of Computer Applications. 2013;**69**

[11] Divya Sree GS, Chandrasekhar P, Venkateshulu B. SVM based speech emotion recognition compared with GMM-UBM and NN. IJESC. 2016;**6**

[12] Melki G, Kecman V, Ventura S, Cano A. OLLAWV: Online learning algorithm using worst-violators. Applied Soft Computing. 2018;**66**:384-393

[13] Pan Y, Shen P, Shen L. Speech emotion recognition using support vector machine. International Journal of Smart Home. 2012;**6**:101-108

[14] Peipei S, Zhou C, Xiong C. Automatic speech emotion recognition using support vector machine. IEEE. 2011;**2**:621-625

[15] Sathit P. Improvement of speech emotion recognition with neural network classifier by using speech spectrogram. International Conference on Systems, Signals and Image Processing (IWSSIP). 2015:73-76

[16] Alex G, Navdeep J. Towards end-to-end speech recognition with recurrent neural networks. In: International Conference on Machine Learning. Vol. 32. 2014

[17] Chen S, Jin Q. Multi-Modal Dimensional Emotion Recognition using Recurrent Neural Networks. Australia: Brisbane; 2015

[18] Lim W, Jang D, Lee T. Speech emotion recognition using convolutional and recurrent neural networks. Asia-Pacific. 2017:1-4

[19] Sara M, Saeed S, Rabiee A. Speech Emotion Recognition Based on a Modified Brain Emotional Learning Model. Biologically inspired cognitive architectures. Elsevier; 2017;**19**:32-38

[20] Yu G, Eric P, Hai-Xiang L, van den HJ. Speech emotion recognition using voiced segment selection algorithm. ECAI. 2016;**285**:1682-1683

[21] Kerkeni L, Serrestou Y, Mbarki M, Mahjoub M, Raoof K. Speech emotion recognition: Methods and cases study. In: International Conference on Agents and Artificial Intelligence (ICAART); 2018

[22] Cabanac M. What is emotion? Behavioural Processes. 2002;**60**(2):69-83

[23] Schacter DL, Gilbert DT, Wegner DM. Psychology (2nd Edition). New York: Worth; 2011

[24] Barrett LF, Russell JA. The Psychological Construction of Emotion. Guilford Publications; 2014

[25] James W. What is an emotion? Mind. 1884;**9**(34):188-205

[26] Boekaerts M. The Crucial Role of Motivation and Emotion in Classroom Learning. The Nature of Learning: Using Research to Inspire Practice 2010. Paris: OECD Publishing; pp. 91-111

[27] Kerkeni L, Serrestou Y, Mbarki M, Raoof K, Mahjoub MA. A review on speech emotion recognition: Case of pedagogical interaction in classroom. In: 2017 International Conference on Advanced Technologies for Signal and Image Processing (ATSIP). IEEE; 2017. pp. 1-7

[28] Ekman P. An argument for basic emotions. Cognition & Emotion. 1992;**6** (3–4):169-200

[29] Matilda S. Emotion recognition: A survey. International Journal of Advanced Computer Research. 2015;**3**(1):14-19

[30] Koolagudi SG, Rao KS. Emotion recognition from speech: A review. International Journal of Speech Technology. 2012;**15**(2):99-117

[31] Schirmer A, Adolphs R. Emotion perception from face, voice, and touch: Comparisons and convergence. Trends in Cognitive Sciences. 2017;**21**(3): 216-228

[32] He C, Yao Yj, Ye Xs. An emotion recognition system based on physiological signals obtained by wearable sensors. In: Wearable Sensors and Robots. Springer; 2017. pp. 15-25

[33] Srinivasan V, Ramalingam V, Arulmozhi P. Artificial Neural Network Based Pathological Voice Classification Using MFCC Features. International Journal of Science, Environment and Technology (Citeseer). 2014;**3**:291-302

[34] Aha DW, Bankert RL. Feature selection for case-based classification of cloud types: An empirical comparison. In: Proceedings of the AAAI-94 Workshop on Case-Based Reasoning. Vol. 106. 1994. p. 112

[35] Song P, Zheng W. Feature selection based transfer subspace learning for speech emotion recognition. IEEE Transactions on Affective Computing. 2018

[36] Duan KB, Rajapakse JC, Wang H, Azuaje F. Multiple SVM-RFE for gene selection in cancer classification with expression data. IEEE Transactions on NanoBioscience. 2005;**4**(3):228-234

[37] Pedregosa F, Varoquaux G, Gramfort A, Michel V, Thirion B, Grisel O, et al. SCIKIT-learn: Machine learning in Python. Journal of Machine Learning Research. 2011;**12**:2825-2830

[38] Guyon I, Weston J, Barnhill S, Vapnik V. Gene selection for cancer classification using support vector

machines. Machine Learning. 2002;**46** (1–3):389-422

[39] Naseem I, Togneri R, Bennamoun M. Linear regression for face recognition. IEEE Transactions on Pattern Analysis and Machine Intelligence. 2010;**32**:2106-2112

[40] Gunn SR. Support vector machines for classification and regression [PhD thesis]. 1998

[41] SVM and Kernel Methods MATLAB Toolbox. Available from: http://asi.insa-rouen.fr/enseignants/~arakoto/toolbox/

[42] Parthasarathy S, Tashev I. Convolutional neural network techniques for speech emotion recognition. In: 2018 16th International Workshop on Acoustic Signal Enhancement (IWAENC). IEEE; 2018. pp. 121-125

[43] Sepp H, Jurgen S. Long Short-term Memory. Neural Computation. 1997;**9**: 1735-1780

[44] Vaudable C. Analyse et reconnaissance des émotions lors de conversations de centres d'appels [PhD thesis]. Université Paris Sud-Paris XI; 2012

[45] Swain M, Routray A, Kabisatpathy P. Databases, features and classifiers for speech emotion recognition: A review. International Journal of Speech Technology. 2018;**21**:1-28

[46] Burkhardt F, Paeschke A, Rolfes M, Sendlmeier W, Weiss B. A Database of German Emotional Speech. INTERSPEECH; 2005

[47] Berlin Database of Emotional Speech. Available from: http://emodb.bilderbar.info/start.html

[48] Berlin Database of Emotional Speech. Available from: http://www.elra.info/en/catalogues/catalogue-language-resources/

Chapter 3

A Case Study of Using Big Data Processing in Education: Method of Matching Members by Optimizing Collaborative Learning Environment

Keiko Tsujioka

Abstract

The purpose of this paper is to optimize the combination of members for collaborative learning that utilized learning management system (LMS), a kind of social media. It is considered that there is a problem of this combinatorial optimization because of various discrete elements in education and it is difficult to find exact solution. Then, we have solved this problem by the method of approximate solution in nursing science class with big data processing, for instance, individual traits, learning outcome, and so on. The result shows continuously learning effects. We will report in this fundamental research how to gather learners' various data and optimize matching members of team by local searching. It might be explained how to solve problems of combinatorial optimization by AI.

Keywords: combinatorial optimization, matching members of team, method of approximate solution, big data processing, collaborative learning, feedforward control, feedback control

1. Introduction

Effective collaborative learning is required in nursing science class because of the shortage of numbers in an aging society with a declining birthrate in Japan. LMS, a kind of social media, which any course members are allowed to connect with all information uploaded by them, such as movies, documents, message and so on, likes a social network system, so called computer supported collaborative learning (CSCL) [1]. This system has been brought into nursing science class in order to prepare for practical training with team members. It seems effective for collaborative learning; however, there happened problems which team members had difficulties interacting with each other. It is supposed that there were problems in their relationship among them. From this reason, we have addressed to find out the method of combinatorial optimization for team members so that students can interact with each other through LMS.

CSCL has been studied by many researchers [2], because collaborative learning is expected to have learning effects through interactive communication among group members [3]. Along with developments of social network, the problems of the relationships between individual and individual and individual and groups or community have become revealed [4]. Koschmann [5] pointed out that it is difficult to find out the solution of CSCL problems because the educational system is related to lots of elements and then complicated. From this point of view, it is considered that finding out the exact solution of combinatorial optimization is not easy because of computational complexity, but approximate solution might be possible to reach better solution by local search [6, 7].

In the field of learning sciences, however, Sawyer said that the innovated reform in education, like scaling up from systems approach, is difficult to succeed [8]. The method of scaling up, for instance, a case of server, improves the whole function of the system not by reforming the sever system but by raising the level of CPU. Dede [9] mentions, although the reform of fast food may transform easily to any restaurants affiliating with a certain franchise, it is difficult to prevail a new type of strategy for instructions even in the same school and obtain general acceptances. Therefore, it is predicted to be unsuccessful cases in Education by scaling up of traditional method, because of its definition which were determined by how much becoming widespread and the level of the reliability.

Upon this, he recognizes the value of successful cases which are given priority to a criterion in a certain context and an adjustment with practical research [10, 11]. The reason of his viewpoint is that it is important to be customized to each educational field because it is difficult to adjust with rapid progress or reform, like vegetation and animals are not able to adjust with their rapid habitant changes. Consequently, Dede [12] said "Examining scalability in the context of his subset of powerful conditions may yield a workable index, but only investigation its feasibility by using real data can determine the potential validity and value of such a measure."

For instance, studies of educational data mining (EDM) have been increasing in quantity and analyzed learners' behavior from various aspects [13] and predicted student performance [14]. The research group of Márquez-Vera [15] has found out the method for predicting dropout students as soon as possible by different data mining approaches with high dimensionality and imbalanced data [16]. Similarly, studies of social network analysis (SNA) have gathered learners' data related to not only behavior but also relationships between small groups and individuals. In the field of social psychology, researchers have been studying about small groups. Guetzkow [17] reported that the conflicts of relationships might be influenced by personality or a sense of value and those of problem solving for projects might be influenced by traits of perception or cognition. In Japan, research groups have continued studying and found out that if conflicts of relationship within groups are lower and those of projects within them are higher, learning effects would be higher. And moreover, the motivation of members would become higher to the next subject [18]. Those results of experiments were outcomes within laboratories and not practical ones; however, it must be a good example of a successful combination of team members.

Sawyer [7] introduced that "scale-up researchers successful strive to improve the implementation with each successive interaction of design-implement-evaluate-redesign cycle." Then, we suppose that it is important to choose successful cases in education when we optimize matching members of team with scale-up method of design-implement-evaluate-redesign cycle.

2. Design

In order to optimize combination of team members, supporters (author) gather various progressing learners' information concerning with practices and analyze them, in other words, big data processing and analysis [19]. Before gathering data, which information and how to gather them will be discussed and planned. Results are returned to the instructors. Supporters explain the results to instructors and learners. Then next, how to improve instructions and learning will be discussed.

2.1 Structure of big data processing system

Big data processing system consisted of the measuring system, the data analysis system, and the results of analysis output system (**Figure 1**). Big data processing system provides instructors students' data which are gathered by the measuring system and analyzed by the analysis system so that they can predict students' behavior as feedforward control.

2.2 Concept of big data processing system

After measuring learner's response (2) (**Figure 2**), those data are uploaded to data analysis system (3). The results of analysis are processed by output system (4). Instructors are able to access to the system of output system anytime in order to check the results of learner's assessment (5).

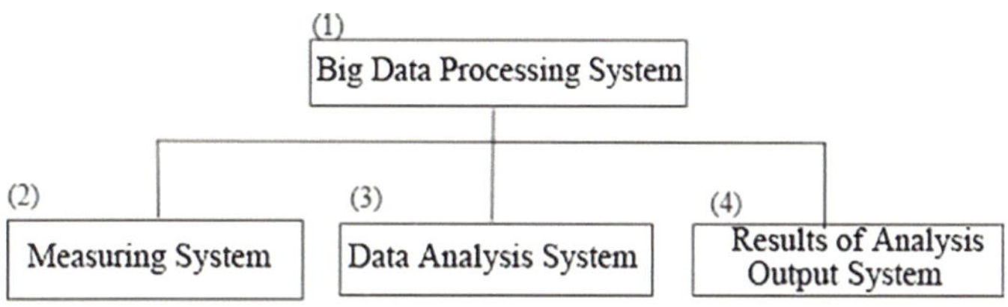

Figure 1.
Big data processing system.

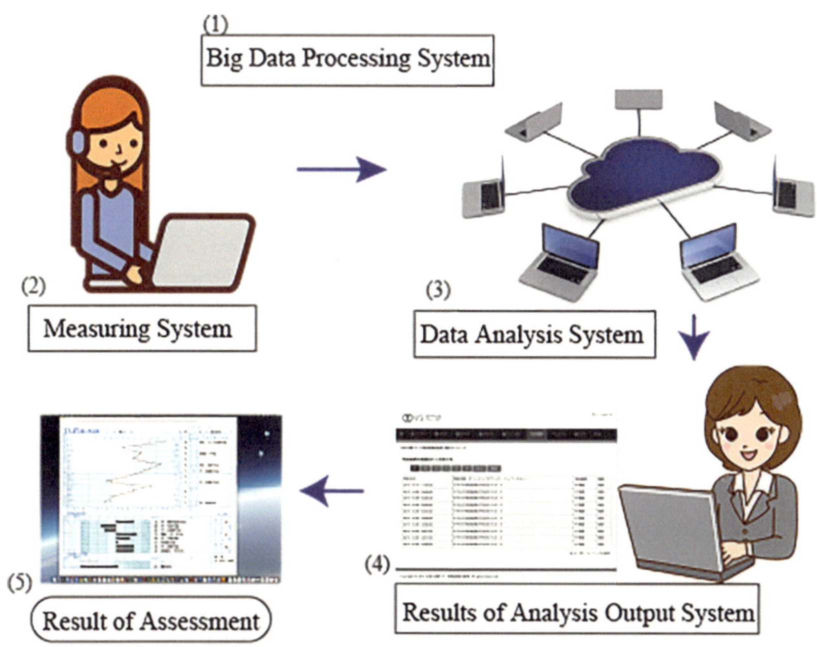

Figure 2.
Concept of big data processing system.

2.2.1 Measuring system

At the stage of the measuring system (2), questionnaires are concerning with personality and presented to participants as a task. Participants are required to solve problems and make decision whether their daily behavior or attitude are similar or not to content of sentences one by one. There are 120 questionnaires which consisted of 20 traits. Each trait has 10 questionnaires which have similar contents to each other. Participants respond to them by selecting answers from yes, no, or neither.

The measuring system will gather information of participants, for instance, attributes, responses, decision time, and so on. Decision time will be measured from the beginning of presenting questionnaires to output information of decisions in which participants selected their response.

There are two ways for presenting questionnaires, sound voice and letters.

Each media presented sentences separately to participants, a total of 240 questionnaires, and gathered information of responses and decision time of each.

2.2.2 Data analysis system

After gathering information by the measuring system, those data will be processed by the data analysis system so that we are able to analyze them, for instance, clustering, categorizing, correlating, and so on, depending on purposes in order to predict behavior and attitude.

2.2.3 Assessment system

In one of the analyses, the results will supply assessments for personality of participants to observers. They will be able to obtain profiles of each participant (Appendix 1). Those profiles show 12 kinds of traits and help the observer to find out characteristics of participants, for example, social introversion, depression, nervousness, and so on. Moreover, from the curved line of the profile, we can categorize personality types, for instance, A to E type.

2.3 Personalized education and learning support system

Instructors (1) (**Figure 3**) need to make an instructional design including grouping and teaming before classes. In this case, they are required to consider learners' individual traits (9) concerning with learning process (4); however, if learners are freshmen (3), instructors have not had enough information about students (2, 5–7) [feedback control A]. Then, individual traits are measured by PELS (10) beforehand (11) [feedforward control] so that instructors can predict learners' behavior and design instructions (12). Because learners are continuously learning (8) [feedback control B] through classes, instructors are required to gather learners' information and redesign instructions. PELS supports them with scale-up method (**Table 1**) [20].

2.4 Hypothesis

1. If relationships among (a–d) members (**Figure 4**) are good and individual traits are different, learning outcomes improve through interactive communication.

2. Instructors are able to find out constrictive conditions of a successful combination of team members through their empirical knowledge about interaction in class (**Figure 5**). They are able to improve combination supported by PELS and continuously obtain learning effects.

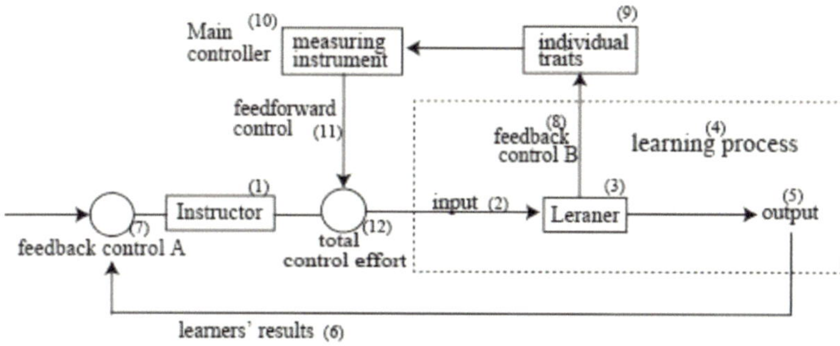

Figure 3.
Model of personalized education and learning support system (PELS).

(1)	Instructor	(7)	feedback control A
(2)	input	(8)	feedback control B
(3)	Learner	(9)	individual traits
(4)	leaning processing	(10)	Main controller (measuring instrument
(5)	output	(11)	feedforward control
(6)	learners' results	(12)	total control effort

Table 1.
Elements of personalized education and learning support system (PELS).

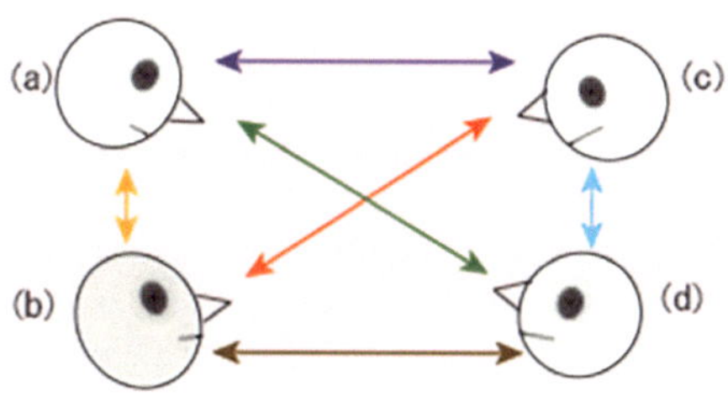

Figure 4.
Model of interaction among team members during collaborative learning.

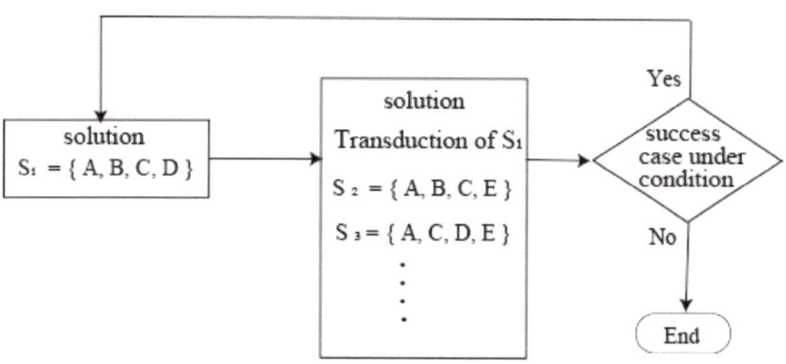

Figure 5.
Local search for solution of combinatorial optimization.

3. Method

3.1 Teacher training

3.1.1 Participants

Participants are 35 female freshmen and 21 sophomores, a total of 56 students. Two instructors participated in the training. Students are divided into teams of four members: freshman, nine teams, and sophomore, six teams.

3.1.2 Duration

Practical research was implemented from April in 2015 to March in 2016. The first semester: 15 classes (90 min each). The second semester: 30 classes (90 min each).

3.1.3 Aims of training

The purpose of the teacher training is to find out the examples of combination of team members.

3.1.4 Procedure

1. Preparing for instructions of prototype practices in nursing science class
   Deciding how to evaluate students' performance

2. Dividing participants into teams consisting of four members each
   Deciding restricted conditions (e.g., avoiding close friends)

3. Implementing practices with team members and evaluating their performance

4. Measuring students' traits by Yatabe-Guilford Personality Inventory (YGPI)

5. Comparing between the results of performance and team combination by personality types

6. Deciding restricted conditions for optimizing combination of team members

3.2 Practical research

3.2.1 Participants

Participants are 98 female freshmen and divided into 25 teams.

3.2.2 Duration

Practical research was implemented from April in 2015 to March in 2016.

The first semester: 15 classes (90 min each). The second semester: 30 classes (90 min each).

3.2.3 Procedure

1. Designing instructions with supporters reflecting the results of prototype practices in teacher training

2. Measuring students' traits by YGPI

3. Dividing participants into 25 teams with four members each (except 2 teams) under restricted conditions which are decided in teacher training

4. Implementing pre-/posttest (low-stakes assessments) which is concerning with conceptual reconstruction related to nursing sciences, before class and end of class

5. Explaining about individual differences to students and instructors by supporters before the first and the second semester

6. Reporting observations in class from instructors to supporters

3.2.4 Data gathering

1. High-stakes assessments: students' performance practiced by traditional method of combination in 2014

2. High-stakes assessments: students' performance practiced by optimizing method of combination in 2015 (e.g., low-stakes assessment; LMS, video, documents, interactive communication, outcomes, reports, questionnaires, and so on).

3.3 Investigation

Duration: from April in 2016 to September in 2018.

Data gathering: high-stakes assessments: students' performance practiced by optimizing method of combination.

Interview: three instructors; one is an expert (a chief instructor); two new members (one is from 2015; the other is from 2017) were asked some questions about an optimization of the combination of team members by an interviewer (an author).

4. Method of analysis

Visualization: comparing between successful and unsuccessful teams by categorization of personality and other factors

Qualitative analysis: comparing between traditional and optimizing methods by analyzing from interview

Quantitative analysis: comparing students' performance (average score) among the passing of years

5. Results

5.1 Results of teacher training

After a prototype practical experiment, students' personality had been measured. Two of nine teams have completed their presentation for freshman, and four of nine teams dropped out. All teams of sophomore have completed and succeeded their presentation. **Figure 6** shows the examples of the relation between performance and combination of team members' personality type. Instructors were required to report their analyses of those relations which teams were success or not from the aspect of not only outcome but also interactive communication during practice. Supporters have explained to instructors about how to understand the results of measurement and help them to predict students' behavior and attitude beforehand [feedforward control].

Then next, they were required to decide on restricted conditions for combinatorial optimization. They have reported:

(1) A type ≧2 or 1; (2) B type <2; (3) C–E type ≦2.

5.2 Results of practical research

Ideally speaking, the method of combinatorial optimization is like **Figure 7**. According to the results of teacher training, types of students' personality were not distributed equally but discrete.

Therefore, we have decided to locally search for a solution of combinatorial optimization along with restricted conditions in which the instructors had found out the rules during teacher training. The results were succeeded, for instance,

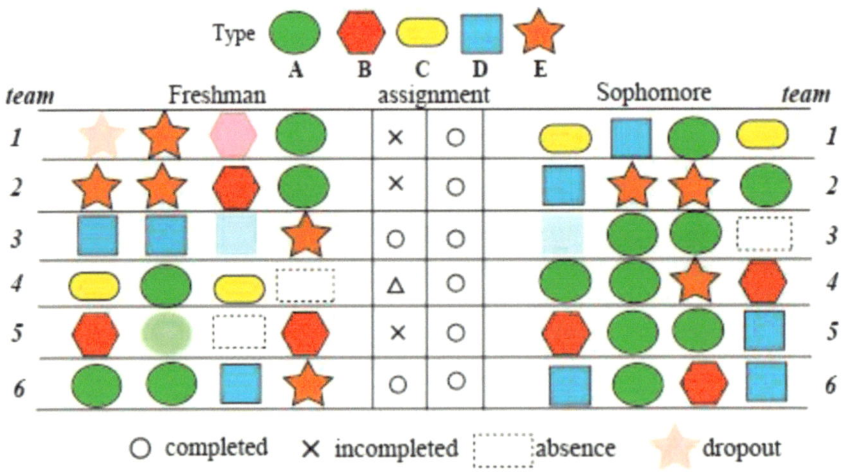

Figure 6.
Comparison of combination among team members by prototype method.

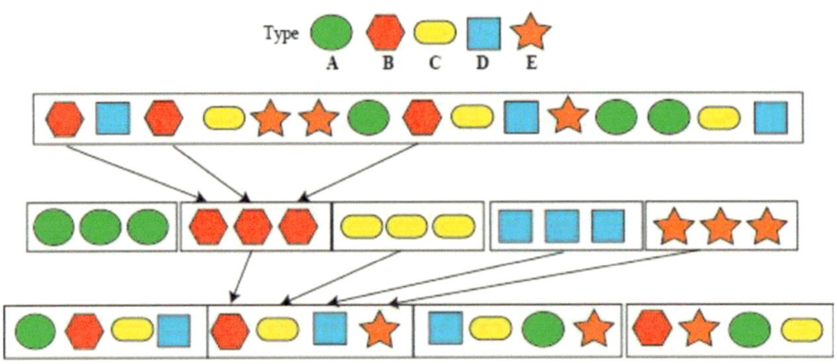

Figure 7.
Model of optimization method of combination under restricted conditions.

all teams have taken out their assignments using LMS, and their average learning outcome (83.95) has become significantly better than those of the previous year (58.94) (df.193, $t = -14.1$, $p < 0.001$). Especially, instructors have reported that their interactive communication had become smooth.

Comparing performance depending on teams in 2015, however, some of them were succeeded but some of them were not. Accordingly, comparing both high- and low-stakes assessments among teams, we have chosen successful and unsuccessful teams, Team B and Team E (**Figure 8**). The combination of members of both teams was satisfied by restricted conditions which instructors had decided.

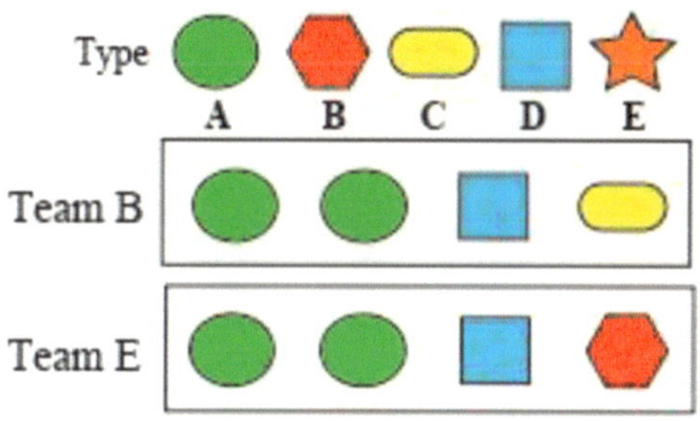

Figure 8.
Comparison of combination between successful and unsuccessful teams: personality types.

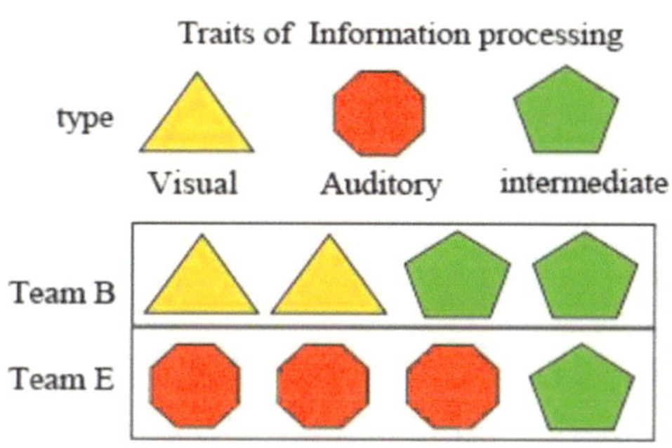

Figure 9.
Comparison of combination between successful and unsuccessful teams: cognitive types.

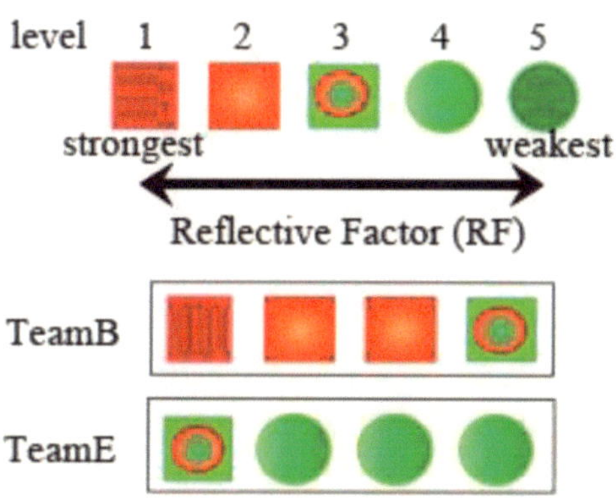

Figure 10.
Comparison of combination between successful and unsuccessful teams: reflective types.

And next, we have analyzed the structure of both team members from the other factors (**Figures 9** and **10**). In both factors, there were unbalances in the combination of Team E. On the other hand, there was a balance in cognitive types for Team B but in reflective factor. In this case, three of them were good at reflection which had effects on their performance.

5.3 Results of investigation

We have carried out a follow-up survey on combinatorial optimization in nursing science class from 2014 to 2018. **Figure 11** shows the results of average scores of high-stakes assessment which were evaluated by the criteria of credits which are required to obtain the qualification of nursing national examination. In the first semester, the average scores have been gradually increased. In contrast, in the second semester, they have been decreasing (**Figure 12**).

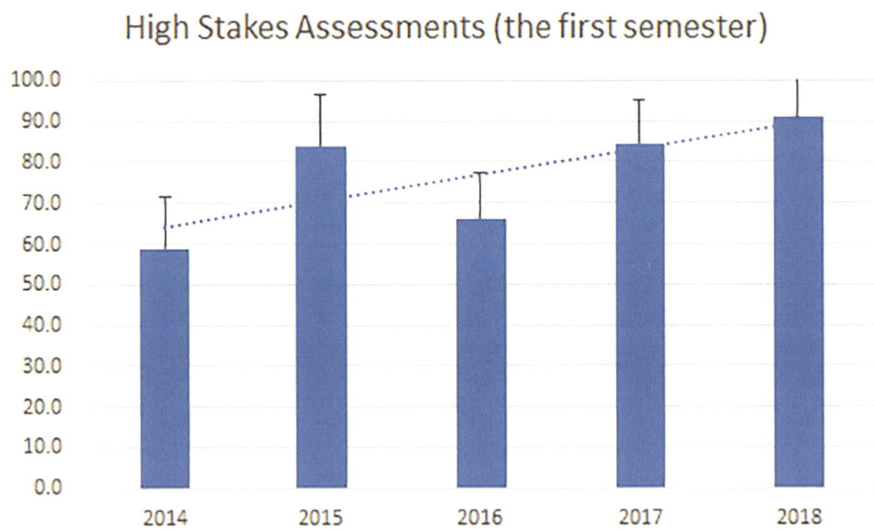

Figure 11.
Changing over the years (from 2014 to 2018).

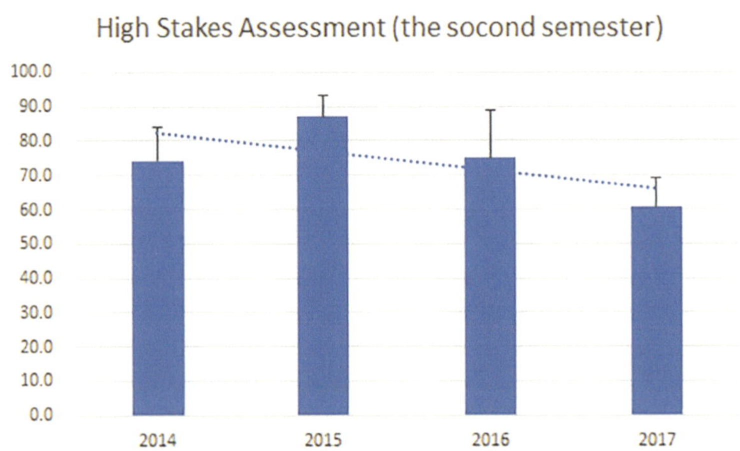

Figure 12.
Changing over the years (from 2014 to 2017).

DOI: http://dx.doi.org/10.5772/intechopen.85526

Three instructors have been interviewed in 2018. The chief instructor has said that she had obtained the method of combination during teacher training. Until then, students had not been able to interact with each other and behaved passive attitude to practice. Other two new members said that they have been referring to the results of measurement of personality while they are teaching. It seems to be a well progression; however, they have not observed the results of personality in detail, for instance, reflective factor and so on.

6. Discussion

We have conducted teacher training and a practical research along with our design (**Figure 3**) in order to examine two hypotheses. The former one, whether learning outcomes improved through interactive communication among team members who were combined by different traits or not, has been examined statistically. The results showed that the average of the traditional method ($n = 97$) in 2014 was 58.9 and those by the optimizing support model (PELS) ($n = 98$) in 2015 was 83.9. The disparity was 25 points, and apparently the results in 2015 were significantly better than those of 2014 (df. = 97, $t = -11.7$, $p < 0.001$) [20].

Moreover, both instructors and supporters have observed that students' behavior and attitude in 2015 were favorable and they have built an excellent relationship. Especially, The members of team B had their interactive communication with each other, even by social network (LMS), and their documents were written out significantly excellently, comparing with those other teams. We have also found that outcomes of Team B had been observed by members of other teams, using LMS. In other words, many of the students had visited to see the documents and conversations of Team B through the network. That is, our optimizing support method might have the synergistic effect, not only within team but also between teams. Although many researchers pointed out the problems about interaction though social network [21], the results of our fundamental research seem fruitful. Then, whether this method might be able to be applied to other cases and how to do it should be discussed.

Then next, the latter hypothesis that an empirical knowledge of instructors helps them to find out the systemic rules of a favorable combination of team members through teacher training should be examined (**Figures 4** and 5). Taken all together,

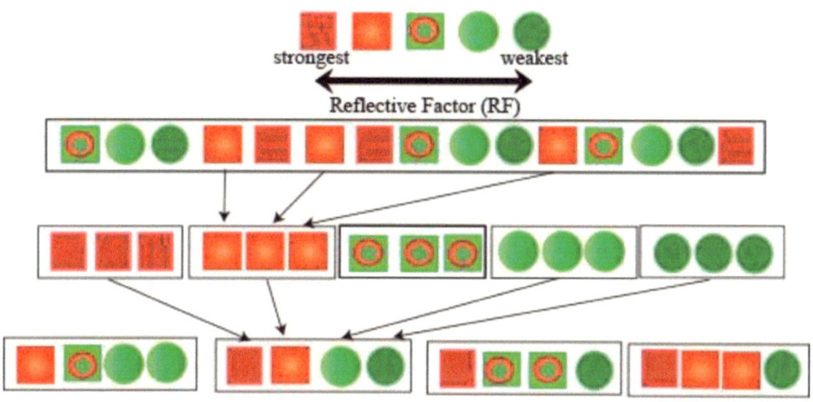

Figure 13.
Model of combinational optimization by reflective factor.

the examination of previous hypothesis has proved an effectiveness of matching members by their optimization. Moreover, the average of students' outcomes in the first semester over the passing of years (from 2015 to 2018) is slightly increasing (**Figure 11**). From this point of view, it is expected learning effectiveness continuously with this method. In contrast, however, there is a slight decrease in the results of the second semester. In addition to this, from the comparison of the results of individual teams, there are successful teams and unsuccessful ones (**Figure 8**). This means, in some extent, their empirical knowledge is recognized by the examination, but some problems of the methodology of optimization remain. The results of comparisons between Team B and Team E (**Figures 9** and **10**) might give us hints of solution. In the case of the second semester, explanations to new instructors and students about categorical visual and auditory types had not been provided in 2017. Concerning with reflective factor, which is one of the evaluations in YGPI, new instructors were also not explained in detail. From those points of view, the problems are caused by insufficient supports.

Look at those issues from different point of views, such as feedforward control and feedback control B (**Figure 3**), in the first semester, the model of optimization by personality types might be an example of a success case, on the other hand, those by other factors might be unsuccessful cases. This means that combinatorial optimization should be supported continuously for instructors and students. This, however, might be an ideal solution; it is supposed that feasibility and machine learning for AI might help us solve this problem with other factors (**Figure 13**). From this aspect, examples of successful and unsuccessful cases might help us to establish algorithm for solution of combinatorial optimization by local searching [22].

7. Conclusions

Computer-supported collaborative learning (CSCL) has begun to be paid attention after progress of social network. Because learners are always able to connect with each other, then learning effect by social interaction is expected. In contrast, many researchers reported the problems concerning with distance communication. In this paper, it is supposed that the problem might be caused by ill combination of team members. Therefore, we have begun to support instructors and students so that they can interact with each other smoothly by using the strategy of approximate solution with the method of scaling up.

We have designed teacher training and practical experiments that utilized personalized education and learning support system (PELS) which is structured by feedforward and feedback control, so that instructors can find out a concrete combinatorial optimization step by step. Consequently, they might have been able to find the method for combination of team members and students' performance had been significantly better than those by traditional method. On the other hand, problems concerning with discrepancies among teams and the example of combinatorial optimization by local search remained, finding transduction of successful team members continuously from a variety of factors. It seems, difficult to practice, however, it is important to develop the method with machine learning by AI.

Acknowledgements

The author is grateful to Dr. Kiyoko Tokunaga and the participants for the collaboration on practical research.

Appendix 1

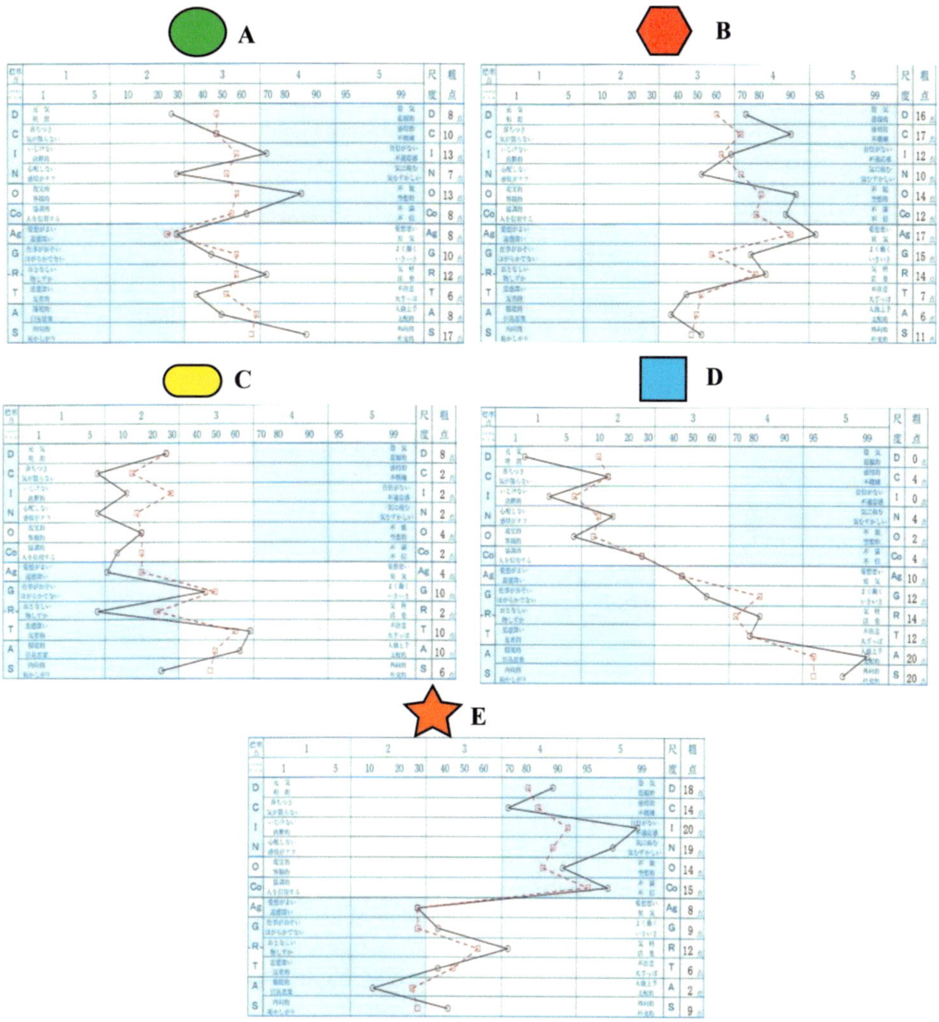

Author details

Keiko Tsujioka
Institute for Psychological Testing, Osaka, Japan

*Address all correspondence to: keiko_tsujioka@sinri.co.jp

IntechOpen

© 2019 The Author(s). Licensee IntechOpen. This chapter is distributed under the terms of the Creative Commons Attribution License (http://creativecommons.org/licenses/by/3.0), which permits unrestricted use, distribution, and reproduction in any medium, provided the original work is properly cited.

References

[1] Stahl G, Koschmann T, Southers DD. Computer supported collaborative learning. In: Sawyer RK, editor. The Cambridge Handbook of the Learning Sciences. Cambridge University Press; 2006. pp. 409-426. ISBN: 100-521-60777-9. paperback

[2] Koschmann T. Paradigm shifts and instructional technology. In: Koschmann T, editor. CSCL: Theory and Practice of an Emerging Paradigm. Mahwah, NJ: Lawrence Erlbaum Associates, Inc; 1996. pp. 1-23

[3] Fransen J, Weinberger A, Kirschner PA. Team effectiveness and team development in CSCL. Educational Psychologist. 2013;**48**(1):9-24. DOI: 10.1080/00461520.2012.747947

[4] Kreijns K, Kirschner PA, Vermeulen M. Social aspects of CSCL environments: A research framework. Educational Psychologist. 2013;**48**(4):229-242. DOI: 10.1080/00461520.2012.750225

[5] Koschmann T. CSCL: Theory and Practice of an Emerging Paradigm. Mahwah, NJ: Lawrence Erlbaum Associates, Inc; 1996

[6] Johnson D. Approximation algorithms for combinatorial problems. Journal of Computer and System Sciences. 1974;**9**:256-278. DOI: 10.1016/S0022-0000(74)80044-9

[7] Crescenzi P, Kann V. Approximation on the web: A compendium of NP optimization problems. In: Rolim J, editor. Randomization and Approximation Techniques in Computer Science. RANDOM 1997. Lecture Notes in Computer Science. Vol. 1269. Berlin, Heidelberg: Springer; 1997

[8] Nathan MJ, Sawyer RK. Foundations of the learning sciences. In: Sawyer RK, editor. The Cambridge Handbook of the Learning Sciences (Second Edition). Cambridge University Press; 2014. pp. 21-42

[9] Clarke J, Dede C, Ketelhut DJ, Nelson B, Bowman C. A design-based research strategy to promote scalability for educational innovations. Educational Technology. 2006;**46**(3):27-36

[10] Nelson BC, Ketelhut DJ, Clark J, Dieterle E, Dede C, Elandson B. Robust design strategies for scaling educational innovations; the river city case study. In: Shelton BE, Wiley D, editors. The Educational Design and Use of Computer Simulation Games. Rotterdam, The Netherlands: Sense Press; 2007. pp. 224-246

[11] Clarke J, Dede C. Design for scalability: A case study of the river city curriculum. Journal of Science Education and Technology. 2009;**18**:353-365. DOI: 10.1007/s10956-009-9156-4

[12] Dede C. Scaling up: Evolving innovations beyond ideal settings to challenging contexts of practice. In: Sawyer RK, editor. The Cambridge Handbook of the Learning Sciences. Cambridge University Press; 2006. pp. 551-565. ISBN: 100-521-60777-9. paperback

[13] Baker R, Simens G. Educational data mining and learning analytics. In: Sawyer RK, editor. The Cambridge Handbook of the Learning Sciences. 2nd ed. Cambridge University Press; 2014. pp. 253-271. ISBN: 100-521-60777-9. paperback

[14] Dutt A, Isamil MA, Herawan T. A Systematic Review on Educational Data Mining, IEEE Access. Vol. 52017. pp. 15991-16005. DOI: 10.1109/ACCESS.2017.2654247. Electronic ISSN: 2169-3536

[15] Márquez-Vera C, Cano A, Romero C, Noaman AYM, Fardoun HM, Ventura S. Early dropout prediction

using data mining: A case study with high school students. Expert Systems. 2016;**3**(1):107-124. DOI: 10.1111/exsy.12135

[16] Márquez-Vera C, Cano A, Romero C, Ventura S. Predicting student failure at school using genetic programming and different data mining approaches with high dimensional and imbalanced data. Applied Intelligence. 2013;**38**(3):315-330. DOI: 10.1007/s10489-012-0374-8

[17] Guetzkow H, Gyr J. An analysis of conflict in decision making groups. Human Relations. 1954;7:367-381

[18] Murayama A, Miura A. Intragroup conflict and subjective performance within group discussion—A multiphasic examination using a hierarchical linear model [In Japanese]. The Japanese Journal of Experimental Social Psychology. 2014;**53**(2):81-92. DOI: 10.2130/jjesp.1203

[19] Tsujioka K. A Case Study of ICT Used by Big Data Processing in Education: Discuss on Visualization of RE Research Paper; ICIET, Association for Computing Machinery; 2018. In printing. ISBN: 978-1-4503-4791

[20] Tsujioka K. Development of Support System Modeled on Robot Suit HAL for Personalized Education and Learning; EITT, Society of International Chinese and Education Technology, IEEE2017. pp. 337-338

[21] Katz N, Lazer D, Arrow H, Contractor N. Network theory and small groups. Small Group Research. 2004;**35**(3):307-332. DOI: 10.1177/1046496404264941

[22] Skansi S. Introduction to Deep Learning: From Logical Calculus to Artificial Intelligence, Computer Science. Springer International Publishing; 2018. ISBN: 978-3-319-73004-2

Chapter 4

Literature Review on Big Data Analytics Methods

Iman Raeesi Vanani and Setareh Majidian

Abstract

Companies and industries are faced with a huge amount of raw data, which have information and knowledge in their hidden layer. Also, the format, size, variety, and velocity of generated data bring complexity for industries to apply them in an efficient and effective way. So, complexity in data analysis and interpretation incline organizations to deploy advanced tools and techniques to overcome the difficulties of managing raw data. Big data analytics is the advanced method that has the capability for managing data. It deploys machine learning techniques and deep learning methods to benefit from gathered data. In this research, the methods of both ML and DL have been discussed, and an ML/DL deployment model for IOT data has been proposed.

Keywords: big data analytics, machine learning, deep learning, big data

1. Introduction

Digital era with its opportunity and complexity overwhelms industries and markets that are faced with a huge amount of potential information in each transaction. Being aware of the value of gathered data and benefitting from hidden knowledge create a new paradigm in this era, which redefines the meaning of power for corporation. The power of information leads organizations toward being agile and to hit the goals. Big data analytics (BDA) enforces industries to describe, diagnose, predict, prescribe, and cognate the hidden growth opportunities and leads them toward gaining business value [68]. BDA deploys advanced analytical techniques to create knowledge from exponentially increasing amount of data, which will affect the decision-making process in decreasing complexity of the process [43]. BDA needs novel and sophisticated algorithms that process and analyze real-time data and result in high-accuracy analytics. Machine and deep learning allocate their complex algorithms in this process considering the problem approach [28].

In this research, a literature review on big data analytics, deep learning and its algorithms, and machine learning and related methods has been considered. As a result, a conceptual model is provided to show the relation of the algorithms that helps researchers and practitioners in deploying BDA on IOT data.

The process of discussing over DL and ML methods has been shown in **Figure 1**.

IntechOpen

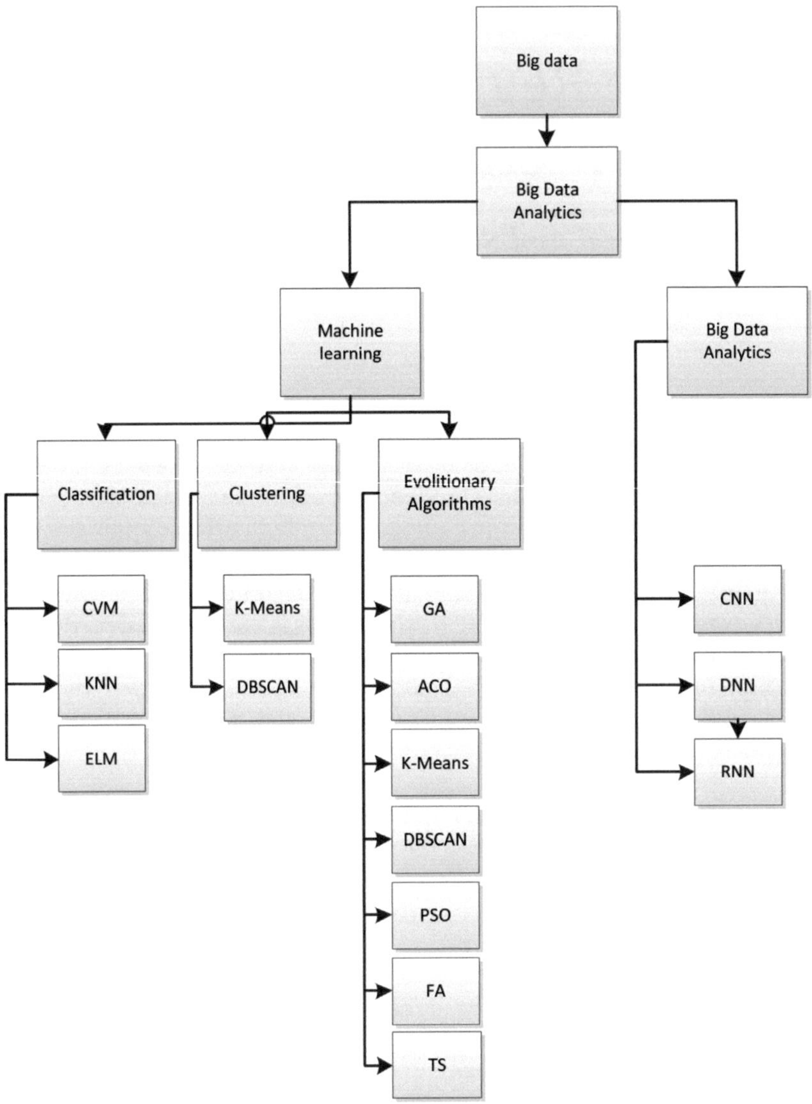

Figure 1.
The big data analytics methods in this research.

2. Big data and big data analytics

One of the vital consequences of the digital world is creating a collection of bulk of raw data. Managing such valuable capital with different shape and size on the basis of organizations' needs the manager's attention. Big data has the power to affect all parts of society from social aspect to education and all in between. As the amount of data increases especially in technology-based companies, the matter of managing raw data becomes much more important. Facing with features of raw data like variety, velocity, and volume of big data entitles advanced tools to overcome the complexity and hidden body of them. So, big data analytics has been proposed for "experimentation," "simulations," "data analysis," and "monitoring." Machine learning as one of the BDA tools creates a ground to have predictive analysis on the basis of supervised and unsupervised data input. In fact, a reciprocal relation has existed between the power of machine learning analytics and data input; the more exact and accurate data input, the more effective the analytical performance. Also, deep learning as a subfield of machine learning is deployed to extract knowledge from hidden trends of data [28].

3. Big data analytics

In digital era with growing rate of data production, big data has been introduced, which is known by big volume, variety, veracity, velocity, and high value. It brings hardness in analyzing with itself which entitled organization to deploy a new approach and tools in analytical aspects to overcome the complexity and massiveness of different types of data (structured, semistructured, and unstructured). So, a sophisticated technique that aims to cope with complexity of big data by analyzing a huge volume of data is known as big data analytics [50]. Big data analytics for the first time was coined by Chen Chiang (2012) who pointed out the relation between business intelligence and analytics that has strong ties with data mining and statistical analysis [11].

Big data analytics supports organizations in innovation, productivity, and competition [16]. Big data analytics has been defined as techniques that are deployed to uncover hidden patterns and bring insight into interesting relations in understanding contexts by examining, processing, discovering, and exhibiting the result [69]. Complexity reduction and handling cognitive burden in knowledge-based society create a path toward gaining advantages of big data analytics. Also, the most vital feature that led big data analytics toward success is feature identification. This means that the crucial features that have important affection on results should be defined. It is followed by identifying of corelations between input and a dynamic given point, which may change during times [69].

As a result of fast evolution of big data analytics, e-business and dense connectivity globally have flourished. Governments, also, take advantages of big data analytics to serve better services to their citizens [69].

Big data in business context can be managed and analyzed through big data analytics, which is known as a specific application of this field. Also, big data gained from social media can be managed efficiently through big data analytics process. In this way, customer behavior can be understood and five features of big data, which are enumerated as volume, velocity, value, variety, and veracity, can be handled. Big data analytics not only helps business to create a comprehensive view toward consumer behavior but also helps organizations to be more innovative and effective in deploying strategies [14]. Small and medium size company use big data analytics to mine their semistructured big data, which results in better quality of product recommendation systems and improved website design [19]. As Ref. [9] cited, big data analytics gains advantages of deploying technology and techniques on their massive data to improve a firm's performance.

According to Ref. [19], the importance of big data analytics has been laid in the fact that decision-making process is supported by insight, which is the result of processing diverse data. This will turn decision-making process into an evidence-based field. Insight extraction from big data has been divided into two main processes, namely data management and data analytics with the former referring to technology support for gathering, storing, and preparing data for analyzing purpose and the latter is about techniques deployed for data analyzing and extracting knowledge from them. Thus, big data analytics has been known as a subprocess of insight extraction. Big data analytics tools are text analytics, audio analytics, video analytics, social media analytics, and predictive analytics. It can be inferred that big data analytics is the main tool for analyzing and interpreting all kinds of digital information [35]. And the processes involved are data storage, data management, data analyzing, and data visualization [9].

Big data analytics has the potential for creating effective and efficient value in both operational and strategic approach for organization and it plays as a game changer in augmenting productivity [20].

Industry practitioners believe that big data analytics is the next 'blue ocean' that brings opportunities for organizations [33], and it is known as "the fourth paradigm of science" [70].

Fields of machine learning (ML) and deep learning (DL) were expanded to deal with BDA. Different fields like "medicine," "Internet of Things (IOT)," and "search engines" deploy ML for exploration of predictive features of big data. In other words, it generalizes learnt patterns to predict future data. Feature construction and data representation are two main elements of ML. Also, useful data extraction from big data is the reason for deploying DL, which is a human-brain inspired technique for processing neural signals as a subfield of ML [28].

4. Big data analytics and deep learning

In 1940s, deep learning was been introduced [71], but the birth of deep learning algorithms has been determined in year 2006 when layer-wise-greedy-learning method was introduced by Hinton to overcome the deficiency of neural network (NN) method in finding optimized point by trapping in optima local point that is exacerbated when the size of training data was not enough. The underlying thought of proposed method by Hinton is to use unsupervised learning before layer-by-layer training happens [72].

Inspiring from hierarchical structure of human brain, deep learning algorithms extract complex hidden features with a high level of abstraction. When massive amounts of unstructured data represent, the layered architecture of deep learning algorithms works effectively. The goal of deep learning is to deploy multiple transformation layers where in every layer output representation is occurred [42]. Big data analytics comprises the whole learnt untapped knowledge gained from deep learning. The main feature of big data analytics, which is extracting underlying features in huge amounts of data, makes it a beneficial tool for big data analytics [42].

Deep learning as a subfield of machine learning has been introduced when some conditions like rise of chip processing, which results in creating huge amounts of data, decreasing computer hardware costs, and noteworthy development in machine learning algorithms were generated. Four categories of deep learning algorithms are as follows:

- convolutional neural networks (CNN)
- restricted Boltzmann machines
- autoencoder
- sparse coding [24]

4.1 Convolutional neural networks (CNN)

CNN inspired from neural network model as a type of deep learning algorithm has a "convolutional layer" and "subsampling layer" architecture. Multi-instance data is deployed as a bag of instances in which each data point is a set of instances [73].

CNN has been known with three features namely "local field," "subsampling," and "weight sharing" and comprised of three layers, which are input, hidden that consists of "convolutional layer" and "subsampling layer" and output layer. In hidden layer, each "convolutional layer" comes after "subsampling layer." CNN training process has been done in two phases of "feed forward" in which the result of previous level entered into next level and "back propagation" pass, which is about modification of errors and deviation through a process of spreading training errors backward and in a hierarchical process [74]. In the first layer, convolution operation is deployed that is to take various filtering phases in each instances, and then, nonlinear transformation function takes place as the result of previous phase transforming into a nonlinear space. After that, the transformed nonlinear space is considered in max-pooling layer, which represents the bag of instances. This step has been done by considering the maximum response of each instance, which was in filtering step. The representation creates a strong pie with the maximum response that can be deployed by predicting instances' status in each class. This will lead to constructing a classification model [73].

CNN is comprised of feature identifier, which is an automatic learning process from extracted features from data with two components of convolutional and pooling layers. Another element of CNN is multilayer perception, which is about taking features that were learned into classification phase [3].

4.2 Deep neural network (DNN)

A deep architecture in supervised data has been introduced with advances in computation algorithm and method, which is called deep neural network (DNN) [3]. It originates from shallow artificial neural networks (SANN) that are related to artificial intelligence (AI) [30].

As hierarchical architecture of DL can constitute nonlinear information in the set of layers, DNN deploys a layered architecture with complex function to deal with complexity and high number of layers [3].

DNN is known as one of the most prominent tools for classifying [49] because of its outstanding classification performance in complex classification matters. One of the most challenging issues in DNN is training performance of it, as in optimization problems it tries to minimize an objective function with high amount of parameters in a multidimensional searching space. So, fining and training a proper DNN optimization algorithm requires in high level of attention. DNN is constructed of structure stacked denoising auto encoder (SDAE) [75] and has a number of cascade auto encoder layers and softmax classifier. The first one deploys raw data to generate novel features, and with the help of softmax, the process of feature classification is performed in an accurate way. The cited features are complementary to each other that helps DNN do its main performance, which is classification in an effective way. Gradient descent (GD) algorithm, which is an optimization method, can be deployed in linear problems with no complex objective function especially in DNN training, and the main condition of this procedure is that the amount of optimization parameter is near to optimal solution [6]. According to Ref. [30], DNN with the feature of deep architecture is deployed as a prediction model [30].

4.3 Recurrent neural network (RNN)

RNN, a network of nodes that are similar to neurons, was developed in 1980s. Each neuron-like node is interconnected with each other, and it can be divided into categories of input, hidden, and output neurons. The data will receive, transform, and generate results in this triple process. Each neuron has the feature of time-varying real-valued activation and every synapse is real-valued weight justifiable [66]. A classifier for neural networks has outstanding performance in not only learning and approximating [105] but also in dynamic system modeling with nonlinear approach by using present data [29, 52]. RNN with the background of human brain–inspired algorithm has been derived from artificial neural network but they are slightly different from each other. Various fields of "associative memories," "image processing," "pattern recognition," "signal processing," "robotics," and "control" have been in the center of focus in research of RNN [67]. RNN with its feedback and feed forward relations can take a comprehensive view from past information and deploy it for adjusting with sudden changes. Also, RNN has the capability of using time-varying data in a recursive way, which simplified the neural network architecture. Its simplicity and dynamic features work effectively in real-time problems [40]. RNN has the ability to process temporal data in hierarchy method and take multilayer of abstract data to show dynamical features, which is another capability of RNN [18]. RNN has the potential to make connection between signals in different levels, which brings significant processing power with huge amounts of memory space [45].

5. Big data analytics and machine learning

Machine learning has been defined as predictive algorithms by data interpretation, which is followed by learning algorithm in an unstructured program. Three main categories of ML are supervised, unsupervised, and reinforcement learning [47], which is done during "data preprocessing," "learning," and "evaluation phase." Preprocessing is related to transformation of raw data into right form that can be deployed in learning phase, which comprises of some levels like cleaning the data, extracting, transforming, and combining it. In the evaluation phase, data set will be selected, and evaluation of performance, statistical tests, and estimation of errors or deviation occur. This may lead to modifying selected parameters from learning process [76]. The first one refers to analyzing features that are critical for classification through a given training data. The data deployed in training algorithm will then become trained and then it will be used in testing of unlabeled data. After interpreting unlabeled data, the output will be generated, which can be classified as discrete or regression if it is continuous. On the other hand, ML can be deployed in pattern identification without training process, which is called unsupervised ML. In this category, when pattern of characteristics are used to group the data, cluster analysis is formed, and if the hidden rules of data have been recognized, another form of ML, which is association, will be formed [77]. In the other words, the main process of unsupervised ML or clustering is to find natural grouping from those data, which is unlabeled. In this process, K cluster in a set number of data is much more similar in comparison with other clusters considering similarity measure. Three categories of unsupervised ML are "hierarchical," "partitioned," and "overlapping" techniques. "Agglomerative" and "divisive" are two kinds of hierarchical methods. The first one is referred to an element that creates a separate cluster with tendency to get involved with larger cluster; however, the second one is a comprehensive set that is going to divide into some smaller clusters. "Partitioned" methods begin with creating several disjoint clusters from data set without considering any hierarchical structure, and "overlapping" techniques are defined as methods that try to find fuzzy or deffuzy partitioning, which is done by "relaxing the mutually disjoint constraint." Among all unsupervised learning techniques, K-means grabs attention. "Simplicity" and "effectiveness" are two main characteristics of unsupervised techniques [47].

5.1 Machine learning and fuzzy logic

Fuzzy logic proposed by Lotfi Zadeh (1965) has been deployed in many fields from engineering to data analysis and all in between. Machine learning also gains advantage from fuzzy logic as fuzzy takes inductive inference. The changes happened in such grounds like "fuzzy rule induction," "fuzzy decision trees," "fuzzy nearest neighbor estimation," or "fuzzy support vector machines" [27].

5.2 Machine learning and classification methods

One of the most critical aspects of ML is classifications [23], which is the initial phase in data analytics [17]. Prior studies found new fields that can deploy this aspect like face recognition or even recognition of hand writing. According to [23], operating algorithm of classification has been divided into two categories: offline and online. In offline approach, static dataset is deployed for training. The training process will be stopped by classifiers after training process is finished and modification of data structured will not be allowed. On the other hand, online category is defined as a "one-pass" type, which is learning from new data. The prominent features of data will be stored in memory and will be kept until the processed training data is erased. Incremental and evolving processes (changing data pattern in unstable environment, which is a result of evolutionary system structure, and continuously updating meta-parameters) are two main approaches for online category [23].

Support vector machine (SVM) was proposed in 1995 by Cortes and Vapnik to solve problems related to multidimensional classification and regression issues as its outstanding learning performance [64]. In this process, SVM constructs a high-dimensional hyperplane that divides data into binary categories, and finding greatest margin in binary categories considering the hyperplane space is the main objective of this method [10]. "Statistical learning theory," "Vapnik-Chervonenkis (VC) dimension," and the "kernel method" are underlying factors of development of SVM [78], which deploys limited number of learning patterns to desirable generalization considering a risk minimization structure [22].

K-nearest neighbor deploys to classify objects in the nearest training class of features [79], and it is known as one of the most widely used algorithms in classification problems in data mining and knowledge extraction. In this method, an object is assigned to its k-nearest neighbors. The efficiency of this method is on the basis of the level of features' weighted qualifications. Some drawbacks of this method are as follows:

- It is highly dependent on the value of K parameter, which is a gauge for determination of neighborhood space.
- The method lacks discrimination ability to differentiate between far and close neighbors.
- Overlapping or noise may happen when neighbor are close [80].

KNN as one of the most important data mining algorithms was first introduced for classification problems, which are expanded to pattern recognition and machine learning research. Expert systems take advantage of KNN classification problems. Three main KNN classifiers that put focus on k-nearest vector neighbor in every class of test sample are as follows:

"Local mean-based k-nearest neighbor classifier (LMKNN)": despite the fact that existing outlier negative influence can be solved by this method, LMKNN is prone to misclassification because of taking single value of k considering neighborhood size per class and applying it in all classes.

"Local mean-based pseudo nearest neighbor classifier (LMPNN)": LMKNN and PNN methods create LMPNN, which is known as a good classifier in "multi-local mean vectors of k-nearest neighbors and pseudo nearest neighbor based on the multi-local mean vectors for each class." Outlier points in addition to k sensitivity have been more considered in this technique. However, differentiation of information in nearest sample of classification cannot recognize widely as weight of all classes are the same [81].

"Multi-local means-based k-harmonic nearest neighbor classifier (MLMKHNN)": MLMKHNN as an extension to KNN takes harmonic mean distance for classification of decision rule. It deploys multi-local mean vectors of k-nearest neighbors per class of every query sample and harmonic mean distance will be deployed as the result of this phase [82]. These methods are designed in order to find different classification decisions [81].

In 2006, Huang et al. proposed extreme learning machine (ELM) as a classification method that works by a hidden single layer feedback in neural network [92]. In this layer, the input weight and deviation will be randomly generated and least square method will be deployed to determine output weight analytically [17], which differentiates this method from traditional methods. In this phase, learning happens followed by finding transformation matrix [93–103]. It is deployed to minimize the sum-of-squares error function. The result of minimizing function will then be used in classification or reduction of dimension [48]. Neural networks are divided into two categories of feed forward neural network and feedback neural networks and ELM is on the first category, which has a strong learning ability specially in solving nonlinear functions with high complexity. ELM uses this feature in addition to fast learning methods to solve traditional feed forward neural network problems in a mathematical change without iteration with higher speed in comparison with traditional neural network [13].

Despite the efficiency of ELM in classification problems, binary classification problems emerge as the deficiency of ELM; as in these problems, a parallel training phase on ELM is needed. In twin extreme learning machine (TELM), the problems will be solved by a simultaneous train and two nonparallel classification hyperplanes, which are deployed for classification. Every hyperplane enters into a minimization function to minimize the distance of it with one class, which is located far away from other classes [60]. ELM is at the center of attention in data stream classification research [83].

5.3 Machine learning and clustering

Clustering as a supervised learning method aims to create groups of clusters, which members of it are in common with each other in characteristics and dissimilar with other cluster members [84]. The calculated interpoint distance of every observation in a cluster is small in comparison with its distance to a point in other clusters [36]. "Exploratory pattern-analysis," "grouping," "decision-making," and "machine-learning situations" are some main applications of clustering technique. Five groups of clustering are "hierarchical clustering," "partitioning clustering," "density-based clustering," "grid-based clustering," and "model-based clustering" [84]. Clustering problems are divided into two categories: generative and discriminative approaches. The first one refers to maximizing the probability of sample generation, which is used in learning from generated models, and the other is related to deploying pairwise similarities, which maximize intercluster similarities and minimize similarities of clusters in between [63].

There are important clustering methods like K-means clustering, kernel K means, spectral clustering, and density-based clustering algorithms that are at the center of research topics for several decades. In K-means clustering, data is assigned to the nearest center, which results from being unable to detect nonspherical clusters. Kernel k-means and spectral clustering create a link between the data and feature space and after that k-means clustering is deployed. Obtaining feature space is done by using kernel function and graph model by kernel k-means and spectral clustering, respectively. Also spectral clustering deploys Eigen-decomposition techniques additionally [26]. K-means clustering works effectively in clustering of numerical data, which is multidimensional [85].

Density-based clustering is represented by DBSCAN, and clusters tend to be separate from data set and be as higher density area. This method does not deploy one cluster for clusters recognition in the data a priori. It considers user-defined parameter to create clusters, which has a bit deviation from cited parameter in clustering process [84].

5.4 Machine learning and evolutionary methods

The main goal of optimization problems is to find an optimal solution among a set of alternatives. Providing the best solution has become difficult if the searching area is large. Heuristic algorithm proposed different techniques to find the optimal solution, but they lack finding the best solution. However, population-based algorithm was generated to overcome the cited deficiency, which is considered to find the best alternative [7].

5.5 Genetic algorithms (GA)

GA is defined as a randomized search, which tries to find near-optimal solution in complex and high-dimensional environment. In GA, a bunch of genes that are called chromosomes are the main parameters in the technique. These chromosomes are deployed as a search space. A number of chromosomes that seem as a collection are called population. The creation of a random population will be followed by representing the goodness degree of objective and fitness function related to each string. The result of this step that will be a few of selected string with a number of copies will be entered into the mating pool. By deploying cross-over and mutation process, a new generation of string will be created from the string. This process will be continued until a termination condition is found. "Image processing," "neural network," and "machine learning" are some examples of application fields for genetic algorithms [38]. GA as nature-inspired algorithm is based on genetic and natural selection algorithms [31].

GA tries to find optimal solution without considering the starting point [104]; also, GA has the potential to find optimal clustering considering clustering metrics [38]. Filter and wrapper search are two main approaches of GA in the field of feature selection. The first one aims to investigate the value of features by deploying heuristic-based data characteristics like correlation, and the second one assesses the goodness of GA solution by using machine learning algorithm [53]. In K-means algorithm, optimized local point is found on the basis of initializing seed values and the generated cluster is on the basis of initial seed values. GA by the aim of finding near-optimal or optimal clustering searches for initial seed values, outperforms K-mean algorithm, and covers the lack of K-mean algorithm [4]. Gaining knowledge from data base is another ground for GA, which plays the role of building "classifier system" and "mining association rules" [58].

Feature selection is a vital problem in big data as it usually contains many features that describe target concepts and chooses proper amount of feature for pre-processing traditionally as a main matter was done by data mining. Feature selection is divided into two groups: independent of learning algorithm, which deploys filter approach, and dependent on learning algorithm, which uses a wrapper approach. However, filter approach is independent of learning algorithm, and the optimal set of feature may be dependent on learning algorithm, which is one of the main drawbacks of filter selection. In contrast, wrapper approach by deploying learning algorithm in evaluation of every feature set works better. A main problem of this approach is complexity in computation field, which is overcome by using GA in feature selection as learning algorithm [56].

5.6 Ant colony optimization (ACO)

Ant colony optimization method was proposed by Dorigo [17] as a population-based stochastic method [15]. The method has been created biologically from real ant behavior in food-seeking pattern. In other words, this bionic algorithm has been deployed for finding the optimal path [44]. The process is that when ants start to seek food they deposit a chemical material on the ground, which is known as pheromone while they are moving toward food source. As the path between the food source and nest become shorter, the amount of pheromone will become larger. New ants in this system tend to choose the path with greater amount of pheromone. By passing time, all ants follow the positive feedback and choose the shortest path, which is signed by greatest amount of pheromone [86]. The applications of ant colony optimization in recent research have been declared as traveling salesman problem, scheduling, structural and concrete engineering, digital image processing, electrical engineering, clustering, routing optimization algorithm [41], data mining [32], robot path planning [87], and deep learning [39].

Some advantages of ant colony optimization method are as follows:

- Less complexity in integration of this method with other algorithms
- Gain advantage of distributed parallel computing (e.g., intelligent search)
- Work better in optimization in comparison with swarm intelligence
- High speed and high accuracy
- Robustness in finding a quasi-optimal solution [41]

As it is stated, the emitted material called pheromone causes clustering between species around optimal position. In big data analytics, ant colony clustering is deployed on the grid board to cluster the data objects [21].

All ant solution constructions, improvement of the movement by local search, and update of the emitted material are involved in a single iteration [23]. So, the main steps of ant colony optimization are as follows:

1. Initializing pheromone trail
2. Deploying pheromone trail to construct solution
3. Updating trail pheromone

On the basis of probabilistic state transition rule, which depends on the state of the pheromone, a complete solution is made by each ant. Two steps of evaporation and reinforcement phase are passed in pheromone updating procedure, where evaporation of pheromone fraction happens and emitting of pheromone that shows the level of solution fitness is determined, respectively, which is followed by finalizing condition [46].

Ant colony decision tree (ACDT) is a branch of ant colony decision that aims to develop decision tress that are created in running algorithm, but as a nondeterministic algorithm in every execution, different decision tree is created. A pheromone trail on the edge and heuristics used in classical algorithm is the principle of ACDT algorithm.

The multilayered ant colony algorithm has been proposed after the disability of one layer ant colony optimization has been declared in finding optimal solution. As an item, value with massive amount of quantity takes too long to grow. In this way, through transactions, maximum quantities of an item is determined and a rough set of membership function will be set, which will be improved by refining process at subsequent levels by reduction in search space. As a result, search ranges will be differing considering the levels. Solution derived from every level is an input for next level, which is considered in the cited approach but with a smaller search space that is necessary for modifying membership functions [88]. Tsang and Kwong proposed ant colony clustering in anomaly detection [65].

5.7 Bee colony optimization (BCO)

BCO algorithm works on inspiration from honey bee's behavior, which is widely used in optimization problems like "traveling salesman problem," "internet hosting center," vehicle routing, and the list goes on. Karaboga in 2005 proposed artificial bee colony (ABC) algorithm. The main features of artificial bee colony (ABC) algorithm are simplicity, easy used and has few elements which need to be controlled in optimization problems. "Face recognition," "high-dimensional gene expression," and "speech segment classification" are some examples that ABC and ACO use to select features and optimize them by having a big search space. In ABC algorithms, three types of bees called "employed bees (EBees)," "onlooker bees (OBees)," and "scout bees deployed" are deployed. In this process, food sources are positioned and then EBees, where their numbers are equal to number of food source, pass the nectar information to OBees. They are equal to the number of EBees. The information is taken to exploit the food source till the finishing amount. Scouts in exhausted food source are employed to search for new food source. The nectar amount is a factor that shows solution quality [25, 55].

This method is comprised of two steps: step forward, which is exploring new information by bees, and step back, which is related to sharing information considering new alternative by bee of hives.

In this method, exploration is started by a bee that tries to discover a full path for its travel. When it leaves the hive, it comes across with random dances of other bees, which are equipped with movement array of other bees that is known as "preferred path." This will lead in foraging process and it comprises of a full path, which was previously discovered by its partner who guides the bee to the final destination. The process of moving from one node to another will be continued till the final destination is reached. For choosing the node by bees, a heuristic algorithm is used, which involves two factors of arc fitness and the distance heuristic. The shortest distance has the possibility to be selected by bees [7]. In BCO algorithm, two values of alpha and beta will be considered, which are exploitation and exploration processes, respectively [8].

5.8 Particle swarm optimization (PSO)

PSO was generated from inspiration from biological organisms, particularly the ability of a grouped animal to work together in order to find the desired location in particular area. The method was introduced by Kennedy and Eberhart in 1995 as a stochastic population-based algorithm, which is known by features like trying to find global optimize point and easy implementation with taking a small amount of parameters in adjusting process. It takes benefit from a very productive searching algorithm, which makes it a best tool to work on different optimization research area and problems [59].

The searching process is led toward solving a nonlinear optimization problem in a real value search space. In this process, an iterative searching happens to find the destination, which is the optimal point. In other words, each particle has a multi-dimensional search with a specific space, which is updated by particle experience or the best neighbor's space and the objective function assesses the fitness value of each particle. The best solution, which is found in each iteration, will be kept in memory. If the optimal solution is found by particle, it is called local best or pbest and the optimal point among the particle neighbors is called global best or gbest [89]. In this algorithm, every potential solution is considered as a particle, which has several features like the current position and velocity. The balance between global and local search can be adjusted by adopting different inertia weight. One of critical success factors in PSO is a trade-off between global and local search in iteration [59]. Artificial neural network, pattern classification, and fuzzy control are some area for deploying PSO [5]. Social interaction and communication metaphor like "birds flock and fish schooling" developed this algorithm and it works on the basis of improving social information sharing, which is done among swarm particles [12].

5.9 Firefly algorithm (FA)

Firefly algorithm was been introduced by Yang [16]. The main idea of FA is that each firefly has been assumed as unisexual, which is attracted toward other firefly regardless of the gender. Brightness is the main attraction for firefly that stimulates the less bright to move toward brighter ones. The attractiveness and brightness are opposed to distance. The brightness of a firefly has been determined by the area of fitness function [90]. As the brightness of firefly increased, the level of goodness of solution increased. A full attraction model has been proposed that shows all fireflies will be attracted to brighter ones and similarity of all fireflies will occur if a great number of fireflies attract to a brighter one, which is measured by fitness value. So, convergence rate during the search method will occur in a slow pace.

FA has been inspired from the lightening feature of fireflies and known as swarm intelligence algorithm. FA better works in comparison with genetic algorithm (GA) and PSO in some cases. "Unit commitment," "energy conservation," and "complex networks" are some examples of working area of FA [61]. Fluctuation may occur when huge numbers of fireflies attract to light emission source and the searching process becomes time-consuming. To overcome these issues, neighborhood attraction FA (NaFA) is introduced, which shows that fireflies are just attracted to only some brighter points, which are outlined by previous neighbor [62].

5.10 Tabu search algorithm (TS)

Tabu search is a meta-heuristic, which was proposed by y Glover and Laguna (1997) on the basis of edge projection and making it better and it tries to make a progress in local search, which leads to a global optimized solution by taking possibility on consecutive algorithm iterations. Local heuristic search process is taken to find solution that can be deployed to combinatorial optimization paradigm [2]. The searching process in this methodology is flexible as it takes adaptive memory. The process is done during different iterations. In each iteration, a solution is found. The solution has a neighbor point that can be reached via "move." In every move, a better solution is found, which can be stopped when no better answer is found [37]. In TS, the aspiration criteria are critical factors that lead the searching process by not considering forbidden solutions that are known by TS. In each solution, the constraints of the objective are met. So, the solutions are both feasible and time-consuming. TS process is continued by using a tabu list (TL), which is a short-term history. The short memory just keeps the recent movement, which is done by deleting the old movement when the memory is full to the maximum level [1].

The main idea of TS is to move toward solution space, which remains unexplored, which would be an opportunity to keep away from local solution. So, "tabu" movements that are recent movements are kept forbidden, which prevents from visiting previous solution points. This is proved that the method brings high-quality solutions in its iterations [57].

6. Big data analytics and Internet of Things (IOT)

Internet of things (IOT) put focus on creating an intelligent environment in which things socialize with each other by sensing, processing, communicating, and actuating activities. As IOT sensors gathered a huge amount of raw data, which is needed to be processed and analyzed, powerful tools will enforce the

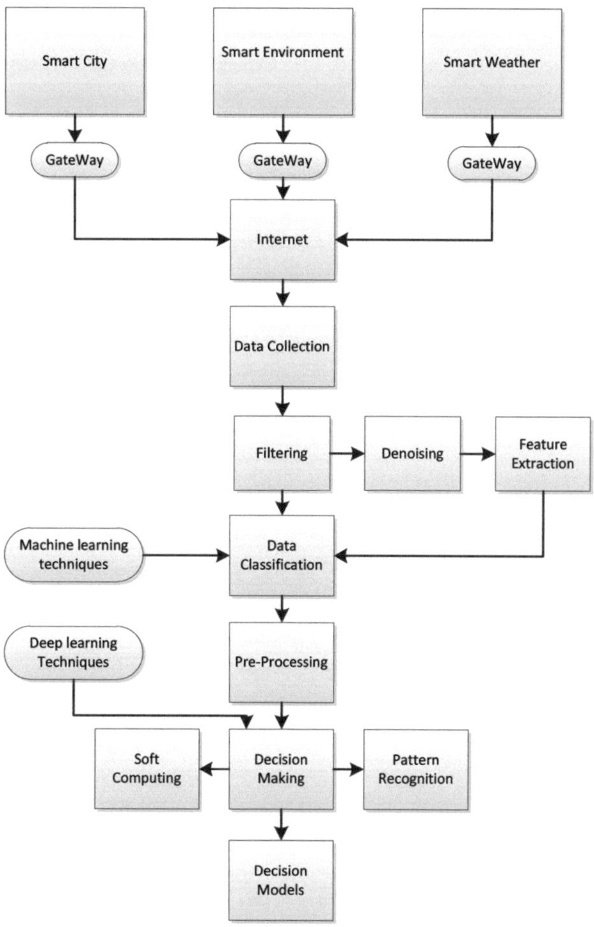

Figure 2.
IOT process.

analytics process. This will stimulate to deploy BDA and its methods on IOT-based data. Ref. [51] proposed a four-layer model to show how BDA can help IOT-based system to work better. This model comprised of data generation, sensor communication, data processing, and data interpretation [51]. It is cited that beyond 2020 cognitive processing and optimization will be considered on IOT data processing [34]. In IOT-based systems, acquired signals from sensors are gathered and deployed for processing in frame-by-frame or batch mode. Also, gathered data in IOT system will be deployed in feature extraction, which is followed by classification stage. Machine learning algorithms will be used in data classifying [54]. Machine learning classification can be deployed on three types of data, which are supervised, semisupervised, and unsupervised [54]. In decision-making level, which is comprised of pattern recognition, deep learning methods, namely, RNN, DNN, CNN, and ANN can be used for discovering knowledge. Optimization process in IOT can be used to create an optimized cluster in IOT data [91].

In **Figure 2**, the process of IOT is shown. Data is gathered from sensors. Data enters the filtering process. In this level, denoising and data cleansing happen. Also, in this level, feature extraction is considered for classification phase. After preprocessing, decision making happens on the basis of deep learning methodology (**Table 1**). Deep learning and machine learning algorithms can be used in analyzing of data generated through IOT device, especially in the classification and decision-making phase. Both supervised and unsupervised techniques can be used in classification phase considering the data type. However, both deep learning and machine learning algorithms are eligible in deploying in decision-making phase.

Phase	Methods		
Classification	Data type	Supervised	SVM
			Logistic regression
			Naïve Bayes
			Linear regression
			k-Nearest neighbors
		Unsupervised	Clustering
			Vector quantization
Decision-making	Deep learning methods		CNN
			RNN
			DNN
			ANN
	Machine learning optimization method		ACO
			GA
			BCO
			FFA
			PSO
			TS

Table 1.
Deep learning and machine learning techniques on IOT phases.

7. Future research directions

For feature endeavors, it is proposed to work on application of big data analytics methods on IOT fog and edge computing. It is useful to extract patterns from hidden knowledge of data gathered from sensors deploying powerful analytical tools. Fog computing is defined as a technology that is implemented in near distance to end user, which provides local processing and storage to support different devices and sensors. Health care systems gain advantage from IOT for fog computing, which supports mobility and reliability in such systems. Health care data acquisition, processing, and storage of real-time data are done in edge, cloud, and fog layer [47]. In future research, the area that machine learning algorithms can provide techniques for fog computing can be on the focus. IOT data captured from smart houses needs analytical algorithms to overcome the complexity of offline and online data gathered in processing, classification, and also next best action, or even pattern recognition [81]. Hospital information system creates "life sciences data," "clinical data," "administrative data," and "social network data." These data sources are overwhelmed with illness predictions, medical research, or even management and control of disease [39]. Big data analytics can be a future subject by helping HIS to cover data processing and disease pattern recognition.

Smart house creates ground for real-time data with high complexity, which entitles big data analytics to overcome such sophistication. Classical methods of data analyzing lost their ability in front of evolutionary methods of classification and clustering. So graphic processing unit (GPU) for machine learning and data mining purposes bring advantage for large scale dataset [7], which leads the applications into lower cost of data analytics. Another way to create future research is to work over different frameworks like Spark, which is an in-memory computation, and with the help of big data analytics, optimization problems can be solved [20].

Deployment of natural language processing (NLP) in text classification can be accompanied by different methods like CNN and RNN. These methods can gain the result with higher accuracy and lower time (Li et al., 2018).

Predictive analytics offered by big data analytics works on developing predictive models to analyze large volume data both structured and unstructured with the goal of identifying hidden patterns and relations between variables in near future [76]. Big data analytics can help cognitive computing, and behavior pattern recognition deploys deep learning technique to predict future action as it is used to predict cancer in health care system [59]. It also leads organizations to understand their problems [13].

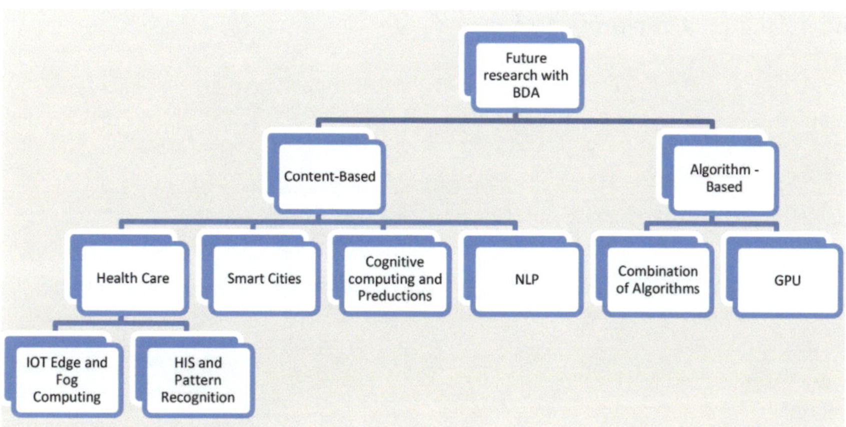

Figure 3.
Future research on big data analytics (BDA).

So, future research can be focused on both the new area for application of different machine learning or deep learning algorithm for censored data gathered and also mixture of techniques that can create globally optimal solution with higher accuracy and lower cost. Researchers can put focus on existing problems of industries through mixed application of machine learning and deep learning techniques, which may results in optimize solution with lower cost and higher speed. They also can take identified algorithms in new area of industries to solve problems, create insight, and identify hidden patterns.

In summary, future research can be done as it is shown in **Figure 3**.

8. Conclusion

This chapter has been attempted to give an overview on big data analytics and its subfields, which are machine learning and deep learning techniques. As it is cited before, big data analytics has been generated to overcome the complexity of data managing and also create and bring knowledge into organizations to empower the performances. In this chapter, DNN, RNN, and CNN have been introduced as deep learning methods, and classification, clustering, and evolutionary techniques have been overviewed. Also, a glance at some techniques of every field has been given. Also, the application of machine learning and deep learning in IOT-based data is shown in order to make IOT data analytics much more powerful in phase of classification and decision-making. It has been identified that on the basis of rapid speed of data generation through IOT sensors, big data analytics methods have been widely used for analyzing real-time data, which can solve the problem of complexity of data processing. Hospital information systems (HIS), smart cities, and smart houses take benefits of to-the-point data processing by deploying fog and cloud platforms. The methods are not only deployed to create a clear picture of clusters and classifications of data but also to create insight for future behavior by pattern recognition. A wide variety of future research has been proposed by researchers, from customer pattern recognition to predict illness like cancer and all in between are comprised in area of big data analytics algorithms.

Acknowledgements

This research received no specific grant from any funding agency in the public, commercial, or not-for-profit sectors.

Author details

Iman Raeesi Vanani and Setareh Majidian*
Information Technology Management, Allameh Tabataba'i University, Iran

*Address all correspondence to: setareh_majidian@atu.ac.ir

IntechOpen

© 2019 The Author(s). Licensee IntechOpen. This chapter is distributed under the terms of the Creative Commons Attribution License (http://creativecommons.org/licenses/by/3.0), which permits unrestricted use, distribution, and reproduction in any medium, provided the original work is properly cited.

References

[1] Bożejko W et al. Parallel tabu search for the cyclic job shop scheduling problem. Computers & Industrial Engineering. 2018;**113**:512-524

[2] Kiziloz H, Dokeroglu T. A robust and cooperative parallel tabu search algorithm for the maximum vertex weight clique problem. Computers & Industrial Engineering. 2018;**118**:54-66

[3] Acharya U et al. Automated detection of coronary artery disease using different durations of ECG segments with convolutional neural network. Knowledge-Based Systems. 2017;**132**:62-71

[4] Babu GP, Murty M. A near-optimal initial seed value selection in K-means algorithm using a genetic algorithm. Pattern Recognition Letters. 1993;**14**(10):763-769

[5] Bonyadi MR, Michalewicz Z. Particle swarm optimization for single objective continuous space problems: A review. Evolutionary Computation. 2017;**25**(1):1-54

[6] Caliskan A et al. Classification of high resolution hyperspectral remote sensing data using deep neural networks. Engineering Applications of Artificial Intelligence. 2018;**67**:14-23

[7] Cano A. A survey on graphic processing unit computing for large-scale data mining. WIREs Data Mining and Knowledge Discovery. 2017;**8**(1):e1232. DOI: 10.1002/widm.1232

[8] Caraveo C et al. Optimization of fuzzy controller design using a new bee colony algorithm with fuzzy dynamic parameter adaptation. Applied Soft Computing. 2016;**43**:131-142

[9] Castillo O, Amador-Angulo L. A generalized type-2 fuzzy logic approach for dynamic parameter adaptation in bee colony optimization applied to fuzzy controller design. Information Sciences. 2018;**460-461**:476-496

[10] Chen J et al. The synergistic effects of IT-enabled resources on organizational capabilities and firmperformance. Information and Management. 2012;**49**(34):140-152

[11] Chou J et al. Metaheuristic optimization within machine learning-based classification system for early warnings related to geotechnical problems. Automation in Construction. 2016;**68**:65-80

[12] Côrte-Real A et al. Assessing business value of Big Data Analytics in European firms. Journal of Business Research. 2017;**70**:379-390

[13] Côrte-Real N et al. Unlocking the drivers of big data analytics value in firms. Journal of Business Research. 2019;**97**:160-173

[14] Delice Y et al. A modified particle swarm optimization algorithm to mixed-model two-sided assembly line balancing. Journal of Intelligent Manufacturing. 2017;**28**(1):23-36

[15] Ding S et al. Extreme learning machine: Algorithm, theory and applications. Artificial Intelligent Review. 2015;**44**(1):103-115

[16] Dong J, Yang C. Business value of big data analytics: A systems-theoretic approach and empirical test. In: Information & Management. 2018. [In Press]

[17] Dorigo M. Ant Colony Optimization: New Optimization Techniques in Engineering. Berlin Heidelberg: Springer-Verlag; 1991. pp. 101-117

[18] Esposito C et al. A knowledge-based platform for Big Data analytics based on publish/subscribe services and stream processing. Knowledge-Based Systems. 2015;**79**:3-17

[19] Feng L et al. Rough extreme learning machine: A new classification method based on uncertainty measure. Neurocomputing. 2019;**325**:269-282

[20] Gonzalez-Lopez J et al. Distributed nearest neighbor classification for large-scale multi-label data on spark. Future Generation Computer Systems. 2018;**87**:66-82

[21] Gallicchio C et al. Deep reservoir computing: A critical experimental analysis. Neurocomputing. 2017;**268**:87-99

[22] Gandomi A, Haider M. Beyond the hype: Big data concepts, methods, and analytics. International Journal of Information Management. 2015;**35**(2):137-144

[23] German F et al. Do retailers benefit from deploying customer analytics? Journal of Retailing. 2014;**90**:587-593

[24] Ghosh A et al. Aggregation pheromone density based data clustering. Information Sciences. 2008;**178**:2816-2831

[25] Gonzalez-Abril L et al. Handling binary classification problems with a priority class by using support vector machines. Applied Soft Computing. 2017;**61**:661-669

[26] Gu X, Angelov P. Self-organizing fuzzy logic classifier. Information Sciences. 2018;**447**:36-51

[27] Guo Y et al. Deep learning for visual understanding: A review. Neurocomputing. 2016;**187**:27-48

[28] Harfouchi F et al. Modified multiple search cooperative foraging strategy for improved artificial bee colony optimization with robustness analysis. Soft Computing. 2017;**22**(19)

[29] Huang J et al. A clustering method based on extreme learning machine. Neurocomputing. 2018;**227**:108-119

[30] Hüllermeier E. Does machine learning need fuzzy logic? Fuzzy Sets and Systems. 2015;**281**:292-299

[31] Jan B et al. Deep learning in big data analytics: A comparative study. Computers and Electrical Engineering. 2017;**75**:1-13

[32] Jiang P, Chen J. Displacement prediction of landslide based on generalized regression neural networks with K-fold cross-validation. Neurocomputing. 2016;**198**:40-47

[33] Jiang S et al. Modified genetic algorithm-based feature selection combined with pre-trained deep neural network for demand forecasting in outpatient department. Expert Systems With Applications. 2017;**82**:216-230

[34] Ko Y. How to use negative class information for Naive Bayes classification. Information Processing and Management. 2017;**53**(6):1255-1268

[35] Koonce D, Tsaib S. Using data mining to find patterns in genetic algorithm solutions to a job shop schedule. Computers & Industrial Engineering. 2000;**38**(3):361-374

[36] Kozak J, Boryczka U. Collective data mining in the ant colony decision tree approach. Information Sciences. 2016;**372**:126-147

[37] Kwon O et al. Data quality management, data usage experience and acquisition intention of big data analytics. International Journal of Information Management. 2014;**34**(3):387-394

[38] Lee I, Lee K. The Internet of Things (IoT): Applications, investments, and challenges for enterprises. Business Horizons. 2015;**58**(4):1-10

[39] Li J et al. Medical big data analysis in hospital information system. In: Big Data on Real-World Applications. 2016. Chapter 4

[40] Loebbecke C, Picot A. Reflections on societal and business model transformation arising from digitization and big data analytics: A research agenda. Journal of Strategic Information Systems. 2015;**24**(3):149-157

[41] Lohrmann C, Luukka P. A novel similarity classifier with multiple ideal vectors based on k-means clustering. Decision Support Systems. 2018;**111**:27-37

[42] Martí R et al. Tabu search for the dynamic bipartite drawing problem. Computers and Operations Research. 2018;**91**:1-12

[43] Maulik U et al. Genetic algorithm-based clustering technique. Pattern Recognition. 2000;**33**(9):1455-1465

[44] Mavrovounioti M, Yang S. Training neural networks with ant colony optimization algorithms for pattern classification. Journal of Soft Computing. 2015;**19**(6):1511-1522

[45] Miao Z et al. Robust tracking control of uncertain dynamic nonholonomic systems using recurrent neural networks. Neurocomputing. 2014;**142**:216-227

[46] Mohan B, Baskaran R. A survey: Ant colony optimization based recent research and implementation on several engineering domain. Expert Systems with Applications. 2012;**39**(4):4618-4627

[47] Mutlag AA et al. Enabling technologies for fog computing in health care IoT systems. Future Generation Computer Systems. 2019;**90**:62-78

[48] Najafabadi M et al. Deep learning applications and challenges in big data analytics. Journal of Big Data. 2015:1-21. DOI: 10.1186/s40537-014-0007-7

[49] Nguyen T et al. Big data analytics in supply chain management: A state-of-the-art literature review. Computers and Operations Research. 2018;**98**:254-264

[50] Ning J et al. A best-path-updating information-guided ant colony optimization algorithm. Information Sciences. 2018;**433-434**:142-162

[51] Osipov V, Osipova M. Space–time signal binding in recurrent neural networks with controlled elements. Neurocomputing. 2018;**308**:194-204

[52] Panda M, Abraham A. Hybrid evolutionary algorithms for classification data mining. In: Neural Computing & Applications. 2014;**26**(3):507-523

[53] Peng H et al. An unsupervised learning algorithm for membrane computing. Information Sciences. 2015;**304**:80-91

[54] Peng Y et al. Orthogonal extreme learning machine for image classification. Neurocomputing. 2017;**266**:458-464

[55] Qawaqneh Z et al. Age and gender classification from speech and face images by jointly fine-tuned deep neural networks. Expert Systems With Applications. 2017;**85**:78-86

[56] Ramsingh J, Bhuvaneswari V. An efficient map reduce-based hybrid NBC-TFIDF algorithm to mine the public sentiment on diabetes mellitus—A big data approach. Journal of King Saud University – Computer and Information Sciences. 2018. [In Press]

[57] Rathore M et al. Urban planning and building smart cities based on the Internet

of Things using Big Data analytics. Computer Networks. 2016;**101**:63-80

[58] Ruan X, Zhang Y. Blind sequence estimation of MPSK signals using dynamically driven recurrent neural networks. Neurocomputing. 2014;**129**:421-427

[59] Sekaran K et al. Deep learning convolutional neural network (CNN) with Gaussian mixture model for predicting pancreatic cancer. Multimedia Tools and Applications. 2019:1-15. DOI: 10.1007/s11042-019-7419-5

[60] Shah S, Kusiak A. Data mining and genetic algorithm based gene/SNP selection. Artificial Intelligence in Medicine. 2004;**31**(3):183-196

[61] Shanthamallu U et al. A brief survey of machine learning methods and their sensor and IoT applications. In: 2017 8th International Conference on Information, Intelligence, Systems & Applications (IISA). 2017. DOI: 10.1109/IISA.2017.8316459

[62] Shunmugapriya P, Kanmani S. A hybrid algorithm using ant and bee colony optimization for feature selection and classification (AC-ABC Hybrid). Swarm and Evolutionary Computation. 2017;**36**:27-36

[63] Sikora R, Piramuthu S. Framework for efficient feature selection in genetic algorithm based data mining. European Journal of Operational Research. 2007;**180**(2):723-737

[64] Silva M, Cunha C. A tabu search heuristic for the uncapacitated single allocation p-hub maximal covering problem. European Journal of Operational Research. 2017;**262**(3):954-965

[65] Srinivasa KG et al. A self-adaptive migration model genetic algorithm for data mining applications. Information Sciences. 2007;**177**(20):4295-4313

[66] Taherkhani M, Safabakhsh R. A novel stability-based adaptive inertia weight for particle swarm optimization. Applied Soft Computing. 2016;**38**:281-295

[67] Wan Y et al. Twin extreme learning machines for pattern classification. Neurocomputing. 2017;**260**:235-244

[68] Wang H et al. Firefly algorithm with neighborhood attraction. Information Sciences. 2017;**382-383**:374-387

[69] Wang H et al. Randomly attracted firefly algorithm with neighborhood search and dynamic parameter adjustment mechanism. Journal of Soft Computing. 2017;**21**(18):5325-5339

[70] Wang Q et al. Local kernel alignment based multi-view clustering using extreme learning machine. Neurocomputing. 2018;**275**:1099-1111

[71] Wu J et al. A patent quality analysis and classification system using self-organizing maps with support vector machine. Applied Soft Computing. 2016;**41**:305-316

[72] Zhang L, Zhang Q. A novel ant-based clustering algorithm using the kernel method. Information Sciences. 2011;**181**:4658-4672

[73] Zhang X et al. An overview of recent developments in Lyapunov–Krasovskii functionals and stability criteria for recurrent neural networks with time-varying delays. Neurocomputing. 2018;**313**:392-401

[74] Zhu S, Shen Y. Robustness analysis for connection weight matrix of global exponential stability recurrent neural networks. Neurocomputing. 2013;**101**:370-374

[75] Wang Y et al. Integrated big data analytics-enabled transformation model: Application to health care. Information and Management. 2018;**55**(1):64-79

[76] Wang Y, Hajli N. Exploring the path to big data analytics success in healthcare. Journal of Business Research. 2017;**70**:287-299

[77] Iqbal R et al. Big data analytics: Computational intelligence techniques and application areas. Technological Forecasting & Social Change. 2018. [In Press]

[78] Wamba S et al. Big data analytics and firm performance: Effects of dynamic capabilities. Journal of Business Research. 2017;**70**:356-365

[79] Zhang Q et al. A survey on deep learning for big data. Information Fusion. 2018;**42**:146-157

[80] Liu W et al. A survey of deep neural network architectures and their applications. Neurocomputing. 2017;**234**:11-26

[81] Yassine A et al. IoT big data analytics for smart homes with fog and cloud computing. Future Generation Computer Systems. 2019;**91**:563-573

[82] Yin Z et al. A-optimal convolutional neural network. Neural Computings & Applications. 2016;**30**(7):2295-2304

[83] Wang S et al. Convolutional neural network-based hidden Markov models for rolling element bearing fault identification. Knowledge-Based Systems. 2018;**144**:65-76

[84] Shi X et al. Tracking topology structure adaptively with deep neural networks. Neural Computing & Application. 2017;**30**(11):3317-3326

[85] Zhou L et al. Machine learning on big data: Opportunities and challenges. Neurocomputing Journal. 2017;**237**:350-361

[86] Tack C. Artificial intelligence and machine learning | applications in musculoskeletal physiotherapy. Musculoskeletal Science and Practice. 2018;**39**:164-169

[87] Tang L et al. A novel perspective on multiclass classification: Regular simplex support vector machine. Information Sciences. 2018;**480**:324-338

[88] Xia M et al. A hybrid method based on extreme learning machine and k-nearest neighbor for cloud classification of ground-based visible cloud image. Neurocomputing. 2015;**160**:238-249

[89] Onan A. A fuzzy-rough nearest neighbor classifier combined with consistency-based subset evaluation and instance selection for automated diagnosis of breast cancer. Expert Systems with Applications. 2015;**42**(20):6844-6852

[90] Gou J et al. A generalized mean distance-based k-nearest neighbor classifier. Expert Systems With Applications. 2019;**115**:356-372

[91] Pan Z et al. A new k-harmonic nearest neighbor classifier based on the multi-local means. Expert Systems With Applications. 2017;**67**:115-125

[92] Xu S, Wang J. Dynamic extreme learning machine for data stream classification. Neurocomputing. 2017;**238**:433-449

[93] Du G et al. Study on density peaks clustering based on k-nearest neighbors and principal component analysis. Knowledge-Based Systems. 2016;**99**:135-145

[94] Yu S et al. Two improved k-means algorithms. Applied Soft Computing. 2018;**68**:747-755

[95] Tabakhi S et al. Gene selection for microarray data classification using a novel ant colony optimization. Neurocomputing. 2015;**168**:1024-1036

[96] Liu H et al. A path planning approach for crowd evacuation in buildings based on improved artificial bee colony algorithm. Applied Soft Computing. 2018;**68**:360-376

[97] Hong T et al. A multi-level ant-colony mining algorithm for membership functions. Information Sciences. 2012;**182**(1):3-14

[98] Kuo RJ et al. Integration of growing self-organizing map and bee colony optimization algorithm for part clustering. Computers & Industrial Engineering. 2018;**120**:251-265

[99] Verma O et al. Opposition and dimensional based modified firefly algorithm. Expert Systems With Applications. 2016;**44**:168-176

[100] Janakiraman S. A hybrid ant colony and artificial bee colony optimization algorithm-based cluster head selection for IoT. Procedia Computer Science. 2018;**143**:360-366

[101] Tsai C et al. Metaheuristic algorithms for healthcare: Open issues and challenges. Computers and Electrical Engineering. 2016;**53**:421-434

[102] Villarrubia G et al. Artificial neural networks used in optimization problems. Neurocomputing. 2018;**272**:10-16

[103] Wari E, Zhu W. A survey on metaheuristics for optimization in food manufacturing. Applied Soft Computing. 2016;**46**:328-343

[104] Wu J et al. Evolving RBF neural networks for rainfall prediction using hybrid particle swarm optimization and genetic algorithm. Neurocomputing. 2015;**148**:136-142

[105] Yang F et al. A new approach to non-fragile state estimation for continuous neural networks with time-delays. Neurocomputing. 2016;**197**:205-211

Chapter 5

Information and Communication-Based Collaborative Learning and Behavior Modeling Using Machine Learning Algorithm

Nityashree Nadar and R. Kamatchi

Abstract

Rapid growth of smart phone industries has led people to use more technology and thus aided in adoption of information and communication technology (ICT) in educational purposes for enhancing students' performance. This chapter shows that students use social media platform or virtual environment for learning, especially in Open University or online learning system. In such environment, the students' drop rate is extremely high. This work primarily aims at reducing students' dropout or students' fails to finish course within prerequisite time using student behavior styles. For addressing research problems, this research aims in building efficient student behavior learning model for improving the performance of student applying machine learning (ML) models. The behavior extraction and study have been carried utilizing decision tree (DT) ML algorithm. Further, a model has been proposed for provisioning student contextual information to different students utilizing VLE platform interaction (collaborative learning) using DT algorithm which considered bagging. The DT with bagging is an ensemble learning (EL) model that depicts bootstrap aggregating (BA), which is modeled for enhancing accuracies and stabilities of every distinct predictive trees. Bagging aids DT in influencing overfitting problems and minimizes its variance. The proposed method is efficient in extracting learning styles and intrinsic behavior of students.

Keywords: behavior modeling, information and communication technology, machine learning, student learning style, virtual learning environment

1. Introduction

This chapter presents collaborative learning model to extract behavior and learning style of students. This chapter describes set of learning style for extracting behavior of students. Further, it also discusses how collaborative learning model aids in designing or understanding behavior of student so as to optimize its training program. Further, this chapter shows how using machine learning aid in increasing accuracy of behavior classification. Along with, presents a student learning style intrinsic behavior classification model using decision tree algorithm with bagging. Mathematical model of proposed decision tree algorithm and decision tree algorithm with bagging is given. Then, the experimental evaluation and result attained by proposed model over existing model is described. Lastly, the overall summary of the chapter is given.

The main objective of this study is to recognize different sorts of ICT teaching methods established in market and determine the role, efficiency and competencies of these practices. The enhancing the ICT practices are characterized as initiatives, activities or projects that have tangible impact on teaching skills and humanizing between learner and trainer. For building an efficient learning model in enhancing performance (i.e., reducing drop rate) of students in academics using ICT [48–50].

Firstly, many analysts explained that learning styles promote that increase in knowledge, and make knowing smoother concerning towards students. Learning handling processed include quite prospering as part of e-learning equal, though a thing executed maybe not incorporate learning trends. Since learning styles should feel secure inside thinking of handling processes, Students 'behavior at the internet Program Requires feel, which is examined or followed. In one of the outset in this work, various programs in which students among various learning models operate in a different way additionally strategy suggestions and different approaches are defined. Second one, emerging approach for the learning styles is proposed by employing machine learning technique. **Figure 1**, depicts concerts Platform Goals and **Figure 2**, the proposed envisioned design is shown. It shows a personalized content delivery of e-learning or online-based learning environment that combine data from student, social media, instructor, classification model [1–3], and content to provision personalized course [6–8].

Secondly, social media has been considered and generally defined as the medium through which information is transmitted among various learners and research communities. This social media platform has been used by various educational institutions for encouraging students to collaboratively learn and interact socially. This work studies and examines the usage of social media in the process of collaborative-based learning using learning algebraic math. In this work, different factors considered to enhancing collaborative learning to study algebra of context

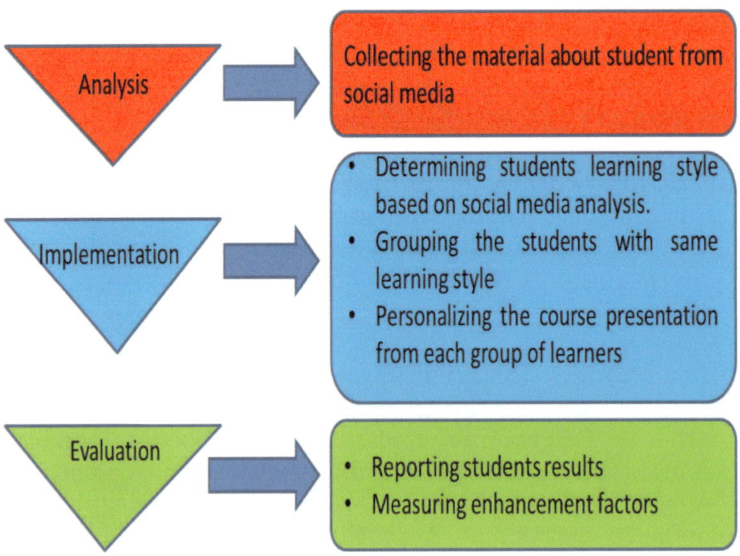

Figure 1.
Proposed framework milestones.

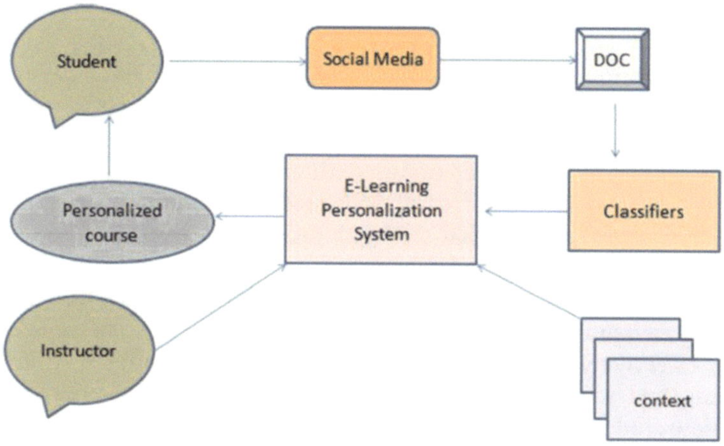

Figure 2.
EMDL (E-learning model design for online learning systems).

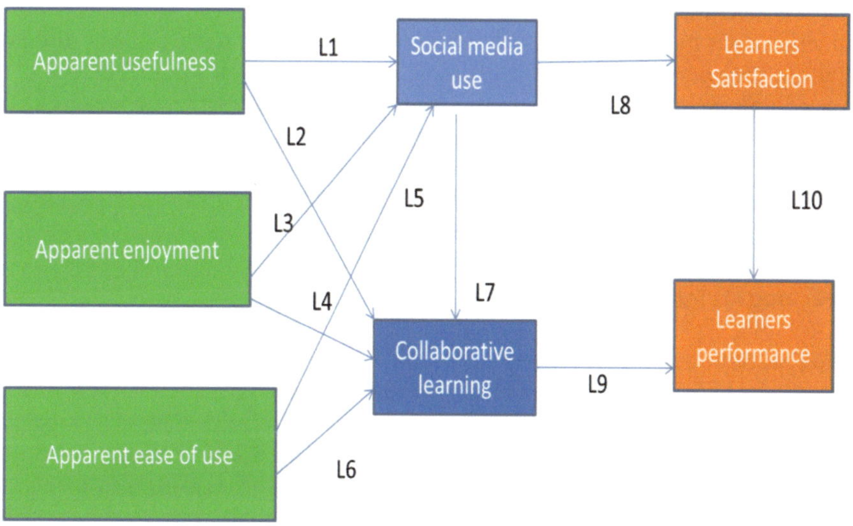

Figure 3.
Proposed hybrid architecture.

using social media are going to be examined. The chapter presents the hybrid research model for ICT education using social media (virtual learning environment) and collaborative learning as shown in **Figure 3**, and the proposed model is analyzed by using machine learning techniques.

2. Proposed collaborative learning using machine learning technique

This section presents proposed collaborative learning model using machine learning technique. Firstly, the behavior and learning style of student are extracted. Then, collaborative learning mechanism using machine learning algorithm using decision tree is presented to accurately extract behavior of student. Lastly, intrinsic behavior of student is extracted using decision tree with bagging method.

2.1 Behavior and earning styles

Regarding learning, this work identified that not all student or person learns in similar manner. A particular set of learning abilities is possessed by each person; thus, the preferences can be identified that constitute his or her learning style. "One size do not fit all" is convey to us by educational research. The learning characteristics of all students differ as informed to us by educational research [9]. Educational research suggests that student's process learns and represents knowledge in different ways, and they prefer to use different type of resources. It is also suggested by the research that it is possible to diagnose students learning style. Further, when instruction is referred to the way they learn some students learn more effectively [10]. Both teacher and students are aided by knowing their learning styles. Teaching and learning strategies can be elaborated better in order to allow students to assimilate in an effective manner and more efficient way in gaining new knowledge and information. To identify and implement better teaching and learning strategies understanding of learning styles can be used [11, 12].

The aforementioned description is a representative of serious mismatches among the teaching style of the instructor and the learning style of student. Students tend to get bored and inattentive, perform poorly on tests, and get discouraged about the course when such a mismatch occurs. This may conclude the students thinking as to withdraw in the subject or course [13]. Some researches in the area of learning styles advocate teaching and learning styles to be matched and bridging the gap between teacher and learners perception in order to reduce teacher's student's style conflicts [14, 15]. This plays an important role enabling students to maximize their classroom experience.

2.2 Learning styles

The theory of learning style depicts the fact that each person has his or her own method or set of Strategies for learning. Preferences strength and characteristic in the way people receive and process information is the definition of a learning style. The strategy may differ from one person to another but it has been narrowed down only up to the GT (Global Trends). The particular ways of learning and this Global trends constitutes the learning style [16]. The trends that all individual have different learning style can be established in a classroom.

Similar lesson has been given to the other student groups, few of them has better performances assured than others students. According to [17], there are several theories about learning styles [17]. Students are classified by a model of learning styles according to a scale that reflects the way the process and receive information. Different learning styles classifies the students, this is done in accordance with the scaling which reflects on similar way as they receive and process the information. Where there is many number of LS tools as well as methodologies [12], two similar assessment equipment's are said to be predominant in the science as well as engineering education Kolb's Learning Styles Inventory (LSI) [18] and the Soloman–Felder Index of Learning Styles (ILS) [11]. For the base of study the fielder and Solomon model was chosen on the study basis of [16] because the other is approved it and it has been implemented in the other work as well [19–21]. Moreover the other researcher [22, 23], because results are easy to interpret and it is user friendly and because the number of dimensions is controlled and can actually be implemented [21].

2.3 Types of behavior and learning style used

The work consider various kinds of learning styles such as active, sensitive, intuitive, visual, global, verbal, reflective, and sequential [5]. Sensitive learning style: Here the courses should poses direct connection with real-time or actual world application content. Intuitive learning style: Here the study material should be designed in theoretical manner with meaning. Along with, it should be innovative with mathematical formula, with proper abstraction and no repetition of content. Visual learning style: here the study material should have lot of visual (i.e., figures and blocks) that depicts certain action. The visualization aid student to remember, understand the concept more easily. Verbal learning style: Here the study material should possess lot of oral presentation with textual data. This kind of student can be given a small abstract to describe or summarize it. Active learning style: Here the learner tends to learn new concept and integrate with practice through discussion. These kind of student should be given assignment in a collaborative manner. Reflexive learning style: This Learning style is based on students' observation and experiences, collection and analyzation of data is done. Prior to making any decision study material must be related with the experiences, personal work must also be included in the requested homework. Sequential learning style: Here the contents are given in steps and chapter wise. The steps or chapter must be logically divided and well connected. Global learning style: Here the assignments are given in random manner. This makes student to think in innovative manner and solve problems in quick manner but may have difficulties to explain how they did it. The above learning styles play an important part in improving student performance.

2.4 Individual and collaborative learning model

Learning style (LS) is characterized as trademark qualities and inclinations in the manners individuals understand and process data [24]. Every student has his/her own method for learning and understanding. However, the most existing model [48–50] is designed for forecasting student drop rate in school. Thus, these model cannot be used online and collaborative environment. In virtual learning environment, student can be separately assisted and their particular requirement can be satisfied through learning process. So as to do that, it is fundamental for VLE platform to keep the data about the students that is viewed as significant for adaptive learning procedure in the student learning environment. Among the student behavior feature sets, used in student learning models, learning styles (LS) comprise a significant environment for improving student specific learning [25–27]. Students gain knowledge from their distinct cooperation/interaction with learning contents; however, they can likewise get information while completing task in collaborative manner with other students. Grouping different individual student based on their characteristic, behavior feature sets using leaning styles can aid in proving the outcome of student learning process [28, 29].

The adaptive learning based on student specific (i.e., based on contextual behavior) is carried out using students learning style, is: (i) sequential students must be straightforwardly assisted through study material, since global students ought to have the option to examine the course in a global manner prior to contemplating certain subjects and (ii) sensing learners will in general like to watch and associate with models prior to learning mathematical ideas or strategies, while instinctive students generally desire the opposite manner. The autonomous grouping is completed in two stages [30]. First, grouping rules decide the clustering arrangement with respect to the individual feature sets and inclinations of the learners. Second, for every collaborative assignment, when it is accessible to a base number of people belongs with similar group, sub-group sets are created and student can start the cooperation/collaboration activity. Similar to many state-of-art model, here we consider the distance metric among individual group member as a significant element for deciding the grouping rules. The final distance is obtained by summing the Euclidean distance (ED), the sensing-intuitive distance and active-reflective distance. For instance, if learner x has gotten the *ILS* score $(x_1 \dots x_2 \dots x_3 \dots x_4)$ and learner y $(y_1 \dots y_2 \dots y_3 \dots y_4)$, the distance D between them is:

$$D = EuclDist + ActRefDist + SenIntDist \tag{1}$$

The Euclidian distance is computed using following equation

$$EuclDist = \sqrt{(x_1 - y_1)^2 + (x_2 - y_2)^2 + (x_3 - y_3)^2 + (x_4 - y_4)^2} \tag{2}$$

Then, the active with respect to reflective distance is computed using following equation

$$ActRefDist = \sqrt{(x_1 - y_1)^2} \tag{3}$$

Similarly, the sensitive with respect to intuitive distance is computed using following equation

$$SenIntDist = \sqrt{(x_1 - y_1)^2} \tag{4}$$

Results, interpreted in many state-of-art models which suggests that the pairs of learners with distance matric greater than the average gets superior outcome results than pairs lower than that. Considering the case, the process for choosing collaborators is to choose arbitrarily the preliminary associate and the at last, compute the farthermost conceivable collaborator to the members of a particular group. However, the learning efficiency can be improved by using machine learning model.

2.5 Using machine learning for obtaining enhanced collaborative learning model

One of the major features that play a critical part in establishing knowledge is learning style. This depicts to the respective student way in which they model a learning assignment. The relation between student behavior and learning styles as online VLE environment or other old-fashioned education frameworks has been investigated by many studies. It is motivating to discover the importance of behavior characteristics of student's practice pattern of this virtual learning environment.

Web-based learning management systems are extensively used nowadays and produce vast amounts of data that are potentially useful for improving educational process [31, 32]. The new evolving area, called Educational Data Mining (EDM), concerns with modeling designs that determine knowledge from information coming from various other sources (traditional or distance learning) environments [33]. Increasing research interests in utilizing DM in teaching is recorded in the last decade [34, 35, 36] with focus on various features of teaching procedures (e.g. teacher, student, study material, etc.). Benefits from extracting knowledge from e-learning data are expected under assumption that the trails of user actions can be used to identify specific information on users. We hope that the user behavior captured in log files and recorded in data structures can be used to create models that predict user behavior, or describe their peculiarities. There are several groups of people who can leverage this knowledge, and are potential stakeholders: Students, Teachers, E-learning system administrators and University management. These stakeholders could use this knowledge for different goals [35]:

- Application that mainly deals with student assessment learning performance.
- Application which gives the Learning recommendation (LR) and Course adoption (CA), these are based on the Student Learning Behavior (SLB).
- Various approaches which deals with learning material evaluation and other educational courses based on the online virtual learning environment.
- Other application which involves the straight feedback for the both students and teachers of e-learning courses; these courses were based on the behavior of student learning.
- Developing the detection nature of a typical student's behavior of learning.

These goals are achieved with the help of data mining techniques such as support vector machines, artificial neural networks, decision trees, k-nearest neighbor, hierarchical clustering, K-means etc. [37]. Since data is not stored in a systematic way as learning management systems (LMS) are not primarily designed with data analysis and Mining in mind. For performing thorough analysis on such data, long and tedious pre-processing is required. Statistical reports are usually produced by LMS systems. Useful conclusions cannot be drawn from this instructions idea for the course potential for student abilities and they are useful only for platform administrative purposes. This chapter describes how one can influence the available data on student learning style and student behavior, in order to forecast success of students, as well as profile students into clusters which may aid in enhancing state-of-art learning content, method, and collaborative learning (CL).

2.6 Using decision tree machine learning algorithm for obtaining enhanced collaborative learning model

The decision tree (DT) is a data mining method or strategy for tackling grouping, classifying and forecasting issues. DT are a basic iterative/recursive building block for communicating a successive classifying operation in which a case, portrayed by a lot of attributes sets, is appointed to one of a disjoint features of classes. DT comprise of nodes (parent) and leaves (child/sibling). Every parent in the tree includes testing a specific characteristic and each leaf of the tree means a class. More often than not, the test contrasts an attributes with a constant. Child nodes give an order that applies to all occurrences that achieve the child, or a classification sets, or a likelihood dispersion over every conceivable clustering. For carrying out classification operation on obscure occasion or condition, it is traversed down the tree as per the estimations of the attributes feature tried in progressive nodes, and when a leaf is achieved, the case is arranged by the class allocated to the leaf. In the event that the property that is tried at a node is an ostensible one, the quantity of siblings is generally the quantity of conceivable estimations of the feature set. The tree intricacy is estimated by one of the accompanying measurements: the all-out number of nodes, complete number of leaves, tree size level and number of feature set utilized [38–41].

As referenced previously, the issue of developing a DT can be communicated iteratively. In the first place, it is important to choose a feature set to put at the root node, and make one branch for every conceivable parameter. This parts up the model set into subsets, one for each estimation of the feature set. Presently the procedure can be rehashed recursively for each branch, utilizing just those cases that really achieve the branch. In the event that whenever all examples at a node have a similar classifying outcome, that piece of the tree needs to end creating [39]. As indicated by [41, 42], the way establishing the feature set that delivers the best split in the information is the one of the primary contrasts among the different DT construction methods.

There are a few method of segmenting/splitting measures. Every DT method utilizes its very own measure to choose among the feature set at each progression while developing or constructing the tree. This work use J48 which is a usage of C4.5 calculation was developed in 1992, by Ross Quinlan, to beat the confinement of the ID3 method (inaccessible qualities, continuous feature set estimation ranges, pruning of DT, and so on.) [43]. C4.5 utilizes a divide-and-conquer way to deal with developing DT. The gain ratio is the default segmenting rule utilized by C4.5, a data-based measure that considers diverse number of test results [44].

$$GR(S,A) = \frac{G(K,H)}{Split\ Info\ (K,H)} \tag{5}$$

where parameter (H) is the set of all conceivable or probable parameter for feature sets H, and K_w is the subset of K for which feature set H has parameter w.

As indicated by [38], the focal decision any tree-based method is choosing which feature set to test at every node in the tree. There is a decent quantifiable metric for this issue, called data or information gain (IG). Yet, so as to characterize IG decisively, it is important to characterize a measure usually utilized in data hypothesis, depicted as entropy, that describes the (im)purity of a self-assertive or random gathering (sets) of models. In the event that the objective characteristic can take on m distinctive parameter, at that point the entropy of K in respect to this m-wise classifying outcome is characterized as [38]:

$$Entropy\ (K) = -\sum_{j=1}^{m} p_j \log_2 p_j \tag{6}$$

where K is an assumed collection set, and p_j is the ratio of K belongs to class label j.

The assumed entropy as a proportion of the (im)purity influence in an accumulation of training models, a proportion of the viability of a feature set in performing classification on training information can be characterized now. The measure is called IG. It is the normal decrease in entropy brought about by apportioning the models as per this quality (feature sets). The IG, $G(K,H)$ of a feature set H, comparing to a dataset of precedents K, is depicted as pursues

$$G(K,H) = Entropy\ (K) - \sum_{w \in parameter(H)} \frac{|K_w|}{K} Entropy\ (K_w) \tag{7}$$

Using proposed decision tree algorithm (machine learning) enhances the collaborative learning efficiency of student behavior and learning styles which is experimentally shown n later section.

2.7 Intrinsic behavior model using proposed decision tree-based classification model

For extracting intrinsic behavior of student, it is important to identify correlation factor among learning styles of students. Further, using correlation measure this work uses decision tree algorithm with bagging to extract intrinsic behavior of student learning style. This work uses decision tree classification algorithm in previous section, however with small optimization introduced. The proposed classification algorithm is an ensemble machine learning (EML) methodology that works by building a large number of DT at training instance and resulting in a classification outcome, which is averaged by each distinct tree [45]. This work uses an additional information or layer of arbitrariness to bagging technique similar to method presented by [47]. Our method will not only performs well for classification and regression function, and at the same time it efficient in identifying behavior [46].

Bagging, which alludes to bootstrap aggregation function, is an ELM method intended to improve the dependability and precision of distinct prescient or forecasting method, for example, trees [47]. Bagging encourages DT to diminish their fluctuation and the impact of overfitting. Considering that a preparation/training dataset is given by $A = a_{1,2\ldots n}$ with response $vB = a_{1,2\ldots n}$, bagging will repeat L instance to choose a self-assertive or random example with substitution of the preparation dataset and fits trees to these feature set sample. A tree i_l, $(L = 1, 2, \ldots L)$ will be trained each instance. Subsequent to preparing, the obtained forecasting method model can be built up by meaning the forecasts from L regression trees (RT) or by taking the greater part vote from L DT. Note that examples are chosen with substitution, and the likelihood that a specific feature set sample isn't chosen after K instance determination can be depicted as follows

$$P = \left(1 - \frac{1}{n}\right)^L \tag{8}$$

In the bagging procedure of proposed grouping (classifying) method, L as a rule equivalents to n. At the point when n is sufficiently enormous, and they are gotten out-of-bags feature set tests.

Furthermore, proposed classification method enhance the universal tree developing method, where at every applicant split in the tree method, an arbitrary subset of the highlights are utilized as opposed to choosing a specific component from every one of the hopefuls. Though in a conventional tree ELM method, if a couple of attributes are solid indicators for the forecasting, these attributes sets will be chosen in a large number of the base estimators. At that point, these trees will be greatly corresponded, hence debilitating the forecast capacities.

The hypothetical foundation of proposed classifying model can be essentially isolated into two sections: RF convergence hypothesis and generalization error limit (GEL). All the evidence of strategy can be obtained from [45]. Subsequently, the convergence of GLE demonstrates that random forest can deliver a restricting estimation of the GE and do not overfit as more trees are included. The upper limit for the GE is obtained using following equation

$$GE \leq \frac{\beta(1 - t^2)}{t^2} \tag{9}$$

where β is the average estimation of the relationship, and t is the quality of a distinct tree in the RF display. It implies that with expanding the quality of distinct tree and lessening the relationship between trees, the proposed classifying method will accomplish progressively exact forecast results.

In addition, as portrayed above, so as to expand the distinct tree quality in the proposed classifying method, attributes set investigation must be first done to decide the overwhelming conduct/learning style for each errand. As it were, good attribute selection, conduct estimations or mix of learning style, firmly identified with every particular conduct must be planned before positioning the attributes sets. At that point, in view of the out-of-bag test sets, every one of the attributes sets can be arranged by the forecast capacity with the out of-bag computes. All the more explicitly, tree-organized classification model in proposed classifier method that have essential factors at nodes should be exceptionally identified with the reaction, so imperative factors can be chosen in these solid trees.

3. Result and analysis

This section evaluates performance evaluation of proposed student behavior (learning style) learning model over existing models. To carry out the experimental analysis, similar to case study (dataset) [5] is considered. However, the dataset is not publically available. As a result, we have generated a dataset similar to [5]. The research work aimed at studying different actions in group (i.e., with different VLE platform). Even though there are different kind of actions in VLE environment, this work have used a total number of actions that majority of learner will carry out on varied VLE platforms. The work studied at predicting behavior and leaning styles of a student that a learner will utilize for collaborating, communicating, and learning assistance. For experiment analysis we have collected data from student considering questionaries' (task) such as presentation, topic discussion etc. More details of dataset can be obtained from Section 3.1 and 3.2. The experiment is conducted using windows 10 OS, 3.2 GHz Intel quad core processor with 16 GB RAM. For extracting behavior, using these collected data ML classifier, using decision tree algorithm is applied. This work use Precision, Recall, ROC, and F-measure to evaluate performance. The precision P^r is computed as follows

$$P^r = \frac{T^p}{T^p + F^p} \tag{10}$$

where T^p is true positive and F^p is false positive.

The recall R^c is computed as follows

$$P^r = \frac{T^p}{T^p + F^n} \tag{11}$$

where F^n is false negative.

The F-measure F is calculated as follows

$$F = \frac{2 * P^r * R^c}{P^r + R^c} \tag{12}$$

Similarly, the ROC is computed as follows

$$ROC = \frac{T^p + T^n}{T^p + T^n + F^p + F^n} \tag{13}$$

where T^n is true negative and F^n is false negative.

The specificity S is calculated as follows

$$S = \frac{T^n}{T^n + F^p} \tag{14}$$

3.1 Problem, issues, and challenges faced in collecting student data

Collecting open source ICT data pertaining to student is challenging. Initially we found difficulties/issues in collecting ICT data of student as there was no any publically available open source dataset. Thus, we have conducted extensive survey of various existing methodology. Form the survey it is evident that many existing methods have manually generated data for extracting learning style of students. Using these styles, the behavior pattern of students is extracted, and the teaching styles are optimized. Further, few model have used social circle for collaborative learning to enhance student behavior. Collecting these kind of data was very much challenging. As a result, we have generated our data for behavior modeling, considering various tasks and assessments. We have collected social circle of various user in Facebook and Twitter and performed collaborative analysis on them. However, it is of very limited use for adopting the student learning performance. Finally, after extensive searching we were able to find an open source data where student online interactions (virtual learning environment) are collected. These data are collected and stored in local hard disk. However, these data have to be anonymized and proper preprocessing steps must be done to support usage of machine learning algorithm on them.

3.2 Data collection for student behavior modeling for conducting experiment analysis

For analysis student learning skills, we have collected student's data, which are composed of data such as number of actions performed for each category (that is, considering different social media platform). The number of actions in this research work has only considered the total number of actions which a student performs on different platforms. Data collection is done considering examining whether it is likely to forecast a student's learning style using their behavior that a student utilizes for communication, collaboration and learning support. Initially, the data is collected considering three kinds of behaviors such as verbal, visual and global. Later, we have collected considering other behavior such as active, reflective, sequential, sensing, and intuitive. Descriptions about each behavior are given in Sections 2.1 and 2.2. The data is collected from students considering questionaries' (task) such as presentation, topic discussion etc. Each student must complete at least one task. Then, the teacher makes assessment of these tasks and gives score that ranges −15 to −15 for different behaviors. Total dataset is composed of 400 student. The sample of data collected is described in **Figure 4**. Further, **Figures 5** and **6** describes the labeled dataset which composed of two classes A and B. Class A depicts the class with positive performance (i.e., score greater than zero) and Class B depicts the class with negative performance (i.e., score lesser than zero). Thus, identifying what type of class aid in improving student learning performance.

3.3 Precision performance evaluation

This section carries out experiment analysis for evaluating performance of proposed classification method using ML over existing ML-based classification method in terms of precision. The **Figure 7**, displays precision result accomplished by

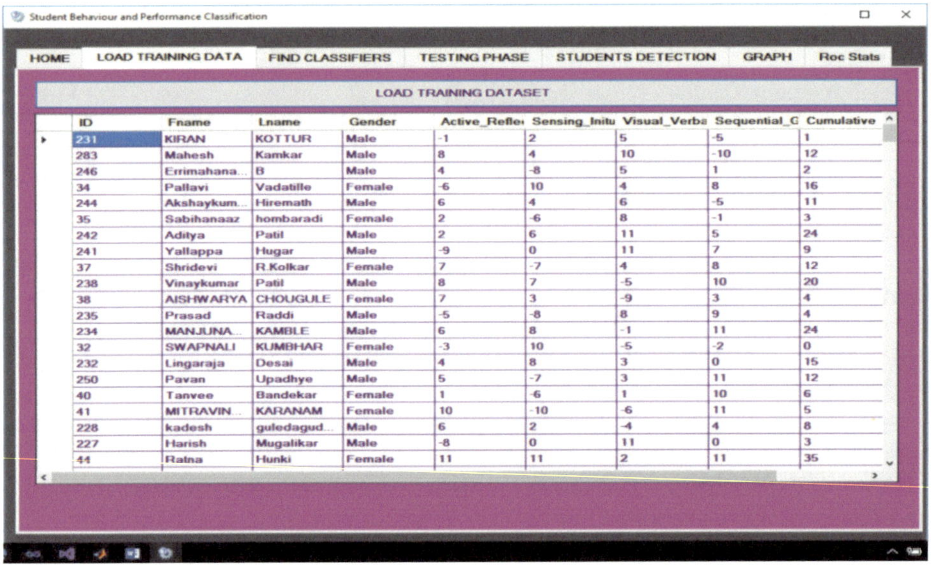

ID	Fname	Lname	Gender	Active_Refle	Sensing_Initu	Visual_Verba	Sequential_G	Cumulative
231	KIRAN	KOTTUR	Male	-1	2	5	-5	1
283	Mahesh	Kamkar	Male	8	4	10	-10	12
246	Errimahana...	B	Male	4	-8	5	1	2
34	Pallavi	Vadatille	Female	-6	10	4	8	16
244	Akshaykum...	Hiremath	Male	6	4	6	-5	11
35	Sabihanaaz	hombaradi	Female	2	-6	8	-1	3
242	Aditya	Patil	Male	2	6	11	5	24
241	Yallappa	Hugar	Male	-9	0	11	7	9
37	Shridevi	R.Kolkar	Female	7	-7	4	8	12
238	Vinaykumar	Patil	Male	8	7	-5	10	20
38	AISHWARYA	CHOUGULE	Female	7	3	-9	3	4
235	Prasad	Raddi	Male	-5	-8	8	9	4
234	MANJUNA...	KAMBLE	Male	6	8	-1	11	24
32	SWAPNALI	KUMBHAR	Female	-3	10	-5	-2	0
232	Lingaraja	Desai	Male	4	8	3	0	15
250	Pavan	Upadhye	Male	5	-7	3	11	12
40	Tanvee	Bandekar	Female	1	-6	1	10	6
41	MITRAVIN...	KARANAM	Female	10	-10	-6	11	5
228	kadesh	guledagud...	Male	6	2	-4	4	8
227	Harish	Mugalikar	Male	-8	0	11	0	3
44	Ratna	Hunki	Female	11	11	2	11	35

Figure 4.
The sample of data collected considering different behaviors of both female and male.

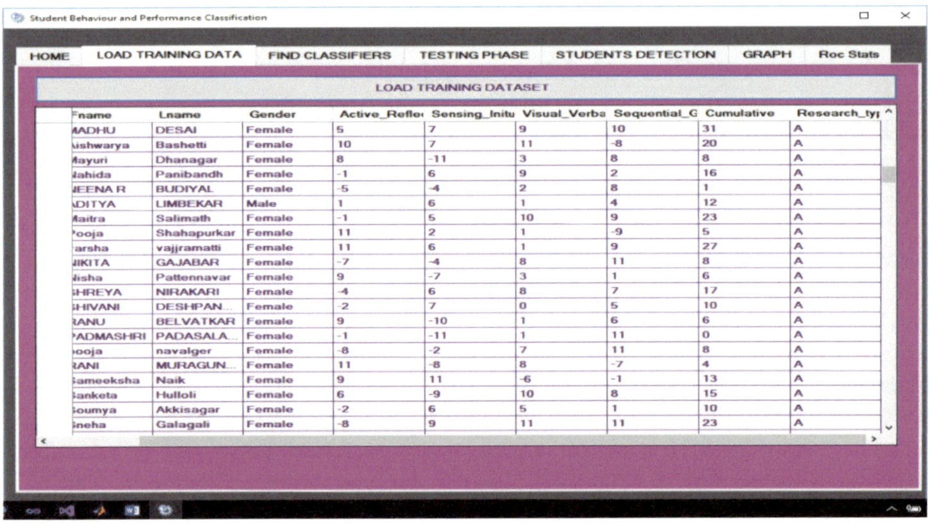

Fname	Lname	Gender	Active_Refle	Sensing_Initu	Visual_Verba	Sequential_G	Cumulative	Research_typ
ADHU	DESAI	Female	5	7	9	10	31	A
ishwarya	Bashetti	Female	10	7	11	-8	20	A
ayuri	Dhanagar	Female	8	-11	3	8	8	A
ahida	Panibandh	Female	-1	6	9	2	16	A
EENA R	BUDIYAL	Female	-5	-4	2	8	1	A
DITYA	LIMBEKAR	Male	1	6	1	4	12	A
aitra	Salimath	Female	-1	5	10	9	23	A
ooja	Shahapurkar	Female	11	2	1	-9	5	A
arsha	vajjramatti	Female	11	6	1	9	27	A
IKITA	GAJABAR	Female	-7	-4	8	11	8	A
isha	Pattennavar	Female	9	-7	3	1	6	A
HREYA	NIRAKARI	Female	-4	6	8	7	17	A
HIVANI	DESHPAN...	Female	-2	7	0	5	10	A
ANU	BELVATKAR	Female	9	-10	1	6	6	A
ADMASHRI	PADASALA...	Female	-1	-11	1	11	0	A
ooja	navalger	Female	-8	-2	7	11	8	A
ANI	MURAGUN...	Female	11	-8	8	-7	4	A
ameeksha	Naik	Female	9	11	-6	-1	13	A
anketa	Hulloli	Female	6	-9	10	8	15	A
oumya	Akkisagar	Female	-2	6	5	1	10	A
neha	Galagali	Female	-8	9	11	11	23	A

Figure 5.
The sample of data collected considering different behaviors of both female and male with binary labeled class (A).

proposed classification method over existing classification method. An average precision performance improvement of 2.07% is attained by proposed classification method over existing classification method. From the results attained, it can be seen that proposed classification method accomplishes superior precision result improvement when compared to existing classification method.

3.4 Recall performance evaluation

This section carries out experiment analysis for evaluating performance of proposed classification method using ML over existing ML-based classification method in terms of recall. The **Figure 8**, shows performance outcome attained by proposed

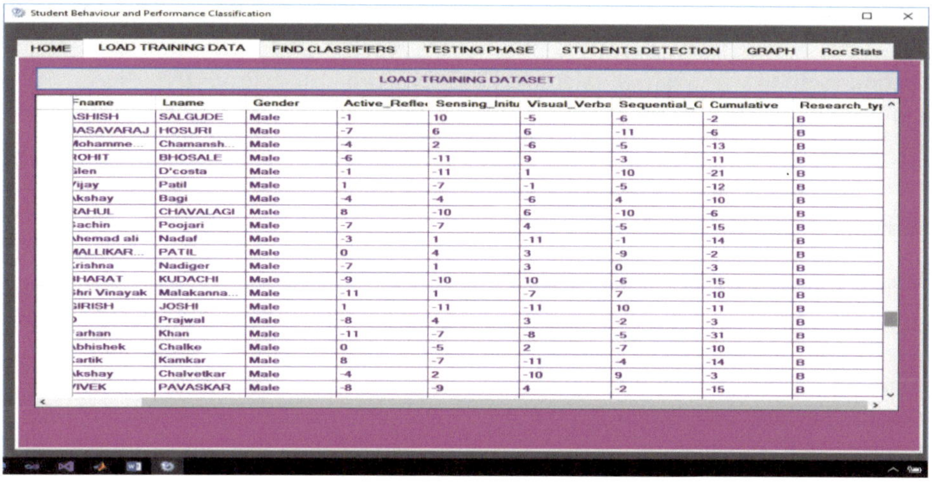

Fname	Lname	Gender	Active_Refle	Sensing_Initu	Visual_Verba	Sequential_G	Cumulative	Research_typ
SHISH	SALGUDE	Male	-1	10	-5	-6	-2	B
ASAVARAJ	HOSURI	Male	-7	6	6	-11	-6	B
ohamme...	Chamansh...	Male	-4	2	-6	-5	-13	B
OHIT	BHOSALE	Male	-6	-11	9	-3	-11	B
len	D'costa	Male	-1	-11	1	-10	-21	B
ijay	Patil	Male	1	-7	-1	-5	-12	B
kshay	Bagi	Male	-4	-4	-6	4	-10	B
AHUL	CHAVALAGI	Male	8	-10	6	-10	-6	B
achin	Poojari	Male	-7	-7	4	-5	-15	B
hemad ali	Nadaf	Male	-3	1	-11	-1	-14	B
ALLIKAR...	PATIL	Male	0	4	3	-9	-2	B
rishna	Nadiger	Male	-7	1	3	0	-3	B
HARAT	KUDACHI	Male	-9	-10	10	-6	-15	B
hri Vinayak	Malakanna...	Male	-11	1	-7	7	-10	B
IRISH	JOSHI	Male	1	-11	-11	10	-11	B
	Prajwal	Male	-8	4	3	-2	-3	B
arhan	Khan	Male	-11	-7	-8	-5	-31	B
bhishek	Chalke	Male	0	-5	2	-7	-10	B
artik	Kamkar	Male	8	-7	-11	-4	-14	B
kshay	Chalvetkar	Male	-4	2	-10	9	-3	B
IVEK	PAVASKAR	Male	-8	-9	4	-2	-15	B

Figure 6.
The sample of data collected considering different behaviors of both female and male with binary labeled class (B).

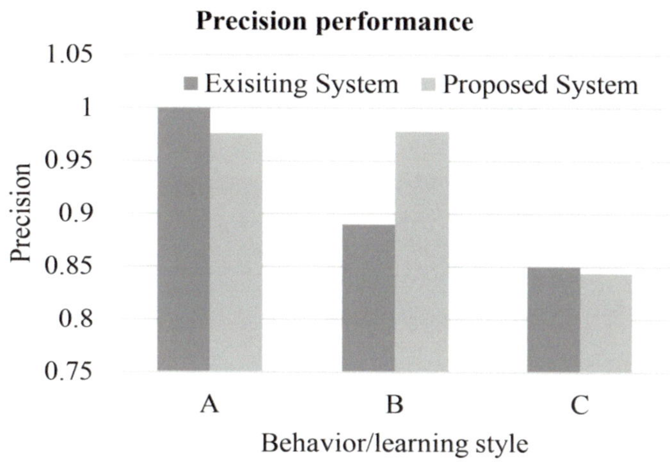

Figure 7.
Precision performance evaluation considering different behavior/learning styles.

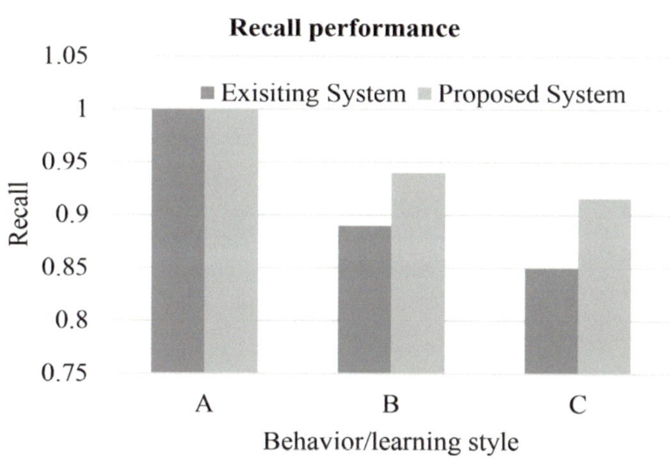

Figure 8.
Recall performance evaluation considering different behavior/learning styles.

classification method and existing classification method in terms of recall. An average recall performance improvement of 3.01% is accomplished by proposed classification method with respect existing classification method. From the results attained, it can be seen, the proposed classification method accomplishes superior recall result improvement than existing classification method.

3.5 F-measure performance evaluation

This section carries out experiment analysis for evaluating performance of proposed classification method using ML over existing ML-based classification method in terms of F-measure. The **Figure 9**, shows F-measure result accomplished by proposed classification method and existing classification method. An average F-measure performance enhancement of 1.53% is accomplished by proposed classification method model with respect to existing classification method. From the results attained, it can be seen the proposed classification method accomplishes superior F-measure result with respect to existing classification method.

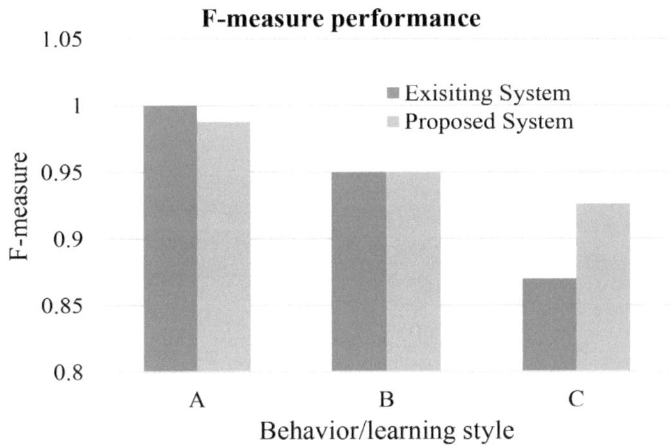

Figure 9.
F-measure performance evaluation considering different behavior/learning styles.

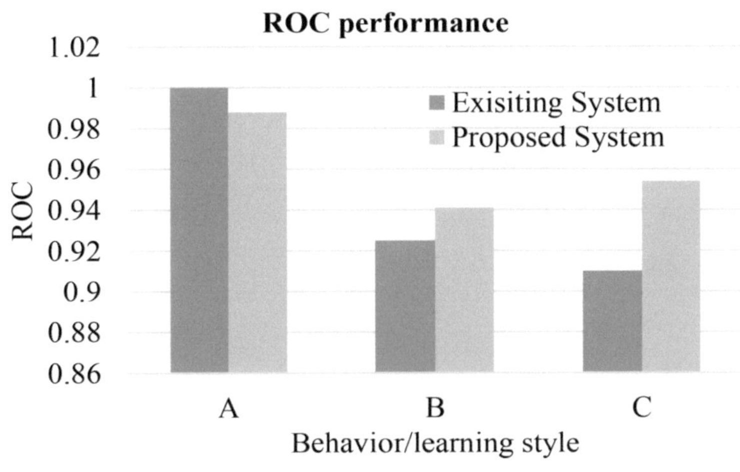

Figure 10.
ROC performance evaluation considering different behavior/learning styles.

3.6 ROC performance evaluation

This section carries out experiment analysis for evaluating performance of proposed classification method using ML over existing ML-based classification method in terms of ROC. The **Figure 10**, displays ROC result accomplished by proposed classification method and existing classification method. An average ROC performance improvement of 1.66% is accomplished by proposed classification method with respect to existing classification method. From the results attained, it can be seen the proposed classification method accomplishes superior ROC results improvement with respect to existing classification method.

3.7 Intrinsic behavior analysis

This section carries out experiment analysis to extract intrinsic behavior of student learning style. We have considered eight behavior style or actions such as

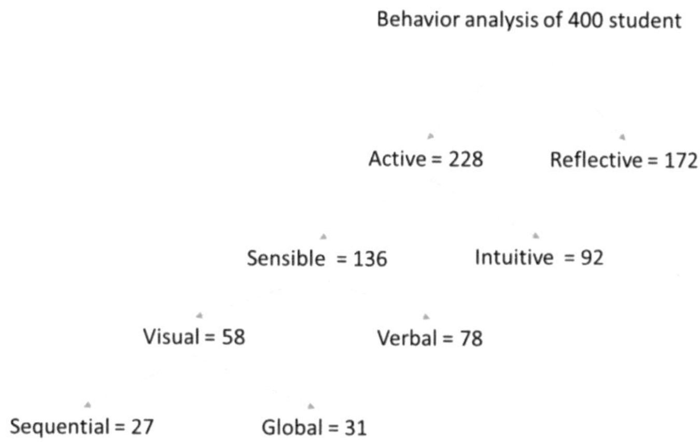

Figure 11.
Decision tree obtained using proposed model to identify how many active students are sensible, visual, sequential and global.

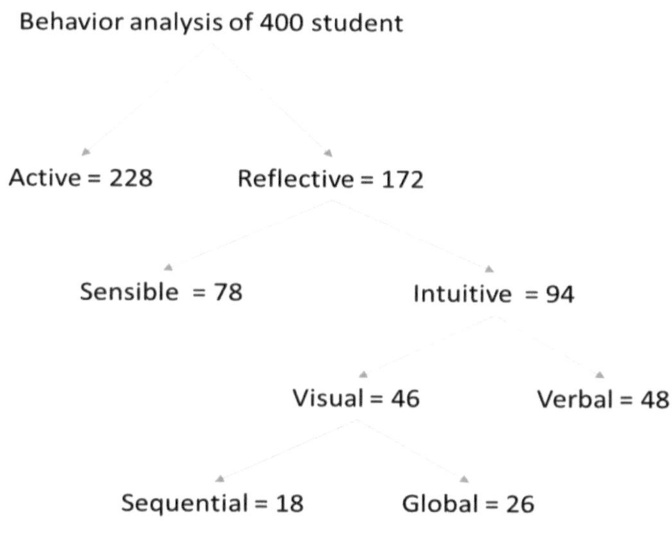

Figure 12.
Decision tree obtained using proposed model to identify how many reflective students are intuitive, visual, sequential and global.

sensing, intuitive, active, reflective, visual, verbal, sequential, and global for experiment analysis. Total dataset composed of 400 students, is used for analysis and experiment is conducted to create decision tree. Various decision tree is built to analyze the behavior and learning style of student as shown in **Figures 11** and **12**. The outcome attained by the proposed model is shown in **Table 1**, and is graphically shown in **Figure 13**. The performance outcome of proposed model over exiting model is shown in T**ables 2–4** considering 100, 200, and 400 students respectively. From the result attained, it can be seen that the proposed model attain good performance. The exiting model did not considered extracting intrinsic behavior of

Reflective	Active	Sensing	Intuitive	Visual	Verbal	Sequential	Global
172	206	196	179	206	183	189	196

Table 1.
Experiment analysis of student learning style.

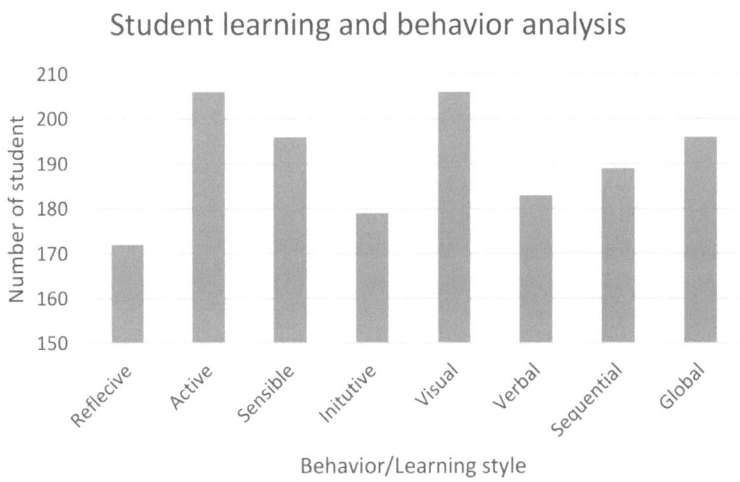

Figure 13.
Student behavior and learning style analysis.

	Accuracy (ROC)	Sensitivity (Recall)	Specificity	Positive prediction (Precision)
Exiting approach [4]	80.6%	79.43%	72.2%	80.17
Our approach	**93.97%**	**91.1%**	**95.3%**	**96.33%**

Table 2.
Algorithm performance evaluation considering 100 students.

	Accuracy (ROC)	Sensitivity (Recall)	Specificity	Positive prediction (Precision)
Exiting approach [4]	81.1%	79.82%	71.96%	81.98
Our approach	**94.17%**	**93.62%**	**96.4%**	**97.32%**

Table 3.
Algorithm performance evaluation considering 200 students.

	Accuracy (ROC)	Sensitivity (Recall)	Specificity	Positive prediction (Precision)
Exiting approach [4]	81.8%	80.24%	71.2%	82.17
Our approach	**95.97%**	**94.6%**	**97.5%**	**98.57%**

Table 4.
Algorithm performance evaluation considering 400 students.

student. However, the proposed model extracts intrinsic behavior of student learning styles. This aid is improving in building better learning model.

4. Conclusions

This chapter firstly discusses the importance, issues, challenges, and problems of using ICT in education. Further, it discusses how collaborative learning using online media enhances or impacts students' learning performance. Then, it also shows that extracting behavior and learning style of student aid enhancing students' performance. The chapter presents an efficient collaborative learning model for enhancing students' performance using machine learning. Experiments are conducted using manually collected dataset. Here we consider only visual, verbal, and global learning styles. The behavior extraction and analysis is done using machine learning such as using decision tree algorithm. Experiment outcome shows that the proposed model improves precision performance by 2.07%, recall performance by 3.01%, F-measure performance by 1.53%, and ROC performance by 1.66% over existing model. The overall results attained shows that the proposed decision tree-based classification model can superiorly extract behaviors and learning styles of students in collaborative manner. Further, the work extracted the intrinsic behavior of student using social media (i.e., online virtual learning environment). This work considers different kinds of behavior or learning style of student such as sensing, intuitive, active, reflective, visual, verbal, sequential, and global for experiment analysis. Experiments are conducted to evaluate the performance of proposed model to extract intrinsic behavior of students. Experiment outcome shows that the proposed model attains Precision (positive predicted value) of 97.4%, Recall (sensitivity) of 93.1%, ROC (Accuracy) of 94.7%, and specificity of 96.4%. The overall result attained shows proposed model attains significant performance over existing model considering extracting intrinsic behavior analysis. Future work would consider building an efficient risk identification model of student fails to complete course on time on Open University and online courses portal.

Author details

Nityashree Nadar[1*] and R. Kamatchi[2*]

1 Information Technology/Computer, S.I.W.S College, Wadala, Mumbai, India

2 ISME school of Management and Research, Mumbai, India

*Address all correspondence to: nityashreenadar@yahoo.co.in and rkamatchiiyer@gmail.com

IntechOpen

© 2019 The Author(s). Licensee IntechOpen. This chapter is distributed under the terms of the Creative Commons Attribution License (http://creativecommons.org/licenses/by/3.0), which permits unrestricted use, distribution, and reproduction in any medium, provided the original work is properly cited.

References

[1] Lakkaraju H, Aguiar E, Shan C, Miller D, Bhanpuri N, Ghani R, et al. A machine learning framework to identify students at risk of adverse academic outcomes. KDD'15 21th ACM SIGKDD International Conference on Knowledge Discovery and Data Mining. 2015: 1909-1918

[2] Bainbridge J, Melitski J, Zahradnik A, Lauria a E, Jayaprakash SM, Baron J. Using learning analytics to predict At-risk students in online graduate public affairs and administration education. The JPAE Messenger. 2015;**21**(2):247-262

[3] Chen T, Guestrin C. Xgboost: A scalable tree boosting system. CoRR, abs/1603.02754; 2016

[4] Raboca HM, Cărbunărean F. Ict in education - exploratory analysis of students' perceptions regarding Ict impact in the educational process. Managerial Challenges of the Contemporary Society. 2014;**7**(2):59

[5] Velázquez F, Lidia A, Cervantes-Pérez F, Saïd A. A quantitative analysis of student learning styles and teacher teachings strategies in a Mexican higher education institution. Journal of Applied Research and Technology. 2012;**10**: 289-308

[6] Kuzilek MH, Zdrahal Z. Open university learning analytics dataset. In: Data Literacy for Learning Analytics Workshop at LAK16, 26th April 2016. Edinburgh, UK; 2016

[7] Hlosta KJ, Zdenek MZ, et al. Scientific Data. 2017;**4**:170171. DOI: 10.1038/sdata.2017.171, 2017

[8] Reigeluth C. A new paradigm of ISD? Educational Technology & Society. 1996;**36**(3):13-20

[9] Honey P, Mumford A. Using your Learning Styles. Maidenhead: Peter Honey; 1986

[10] Rasmussen K. Hypermedia and learning styles: Can performance be influenced? Journal of Multimedia and Hypermedia. 1998;**7**(4):291-308

[11] Felder R. Soloman B. Learning styles and strategies, North Carolina State University [online]. 1993. Available from: http://www.ncsu.edu/felderpublic/ILSdir/ILS.pdf [Accessed on 28-05-2007]

[12] Coffield F, Moseley D, Hall E, Ecclestone K. Learning styles and pedagogy in post–16 learning: A systematic and critical review, Learning and Skills Research Center Report [online]. 2004. Available from: www.LSRC.ac.uk.

[13] Oxford R, Ehrman M, Lavine R. Style wars: Teacher-student style conflicts in the language classroom. In: Magnan S, editor. Challenges in the 1990's for College Foreign Language Programs. Boston: Heinle and Heinle; 1991

[14] Smith L, Renzulli J. Learning style preference: A practical approach for classroom teachers. Theory Into Practice. 1984;**23**(1):45-50

[15] Charkins R, O'Toole D, Wetzel J. Linking teacher and student learning styles with student achievement and attitudes. The Journal of Economic Education. 1985;**16**:111-120

[16] Felder R, Silverman L. Learning and teaching styles in engineering education. Engineering Education. 1988; **78**:674-681

[17] Sewall T. The measurement of learning style: A critique of four assessment tools. ERIC ED267247; 1986

[18] Kolb D. Experimental Learning: Experience as the Source of Learning and Development. Englewood Cliffs, NJ: Prentice-Hall; 1984

[19] Carver C, Howard R, Lane W. Enhancing student learning through hypermedia courseware and incorporation of student learning styles. IEEE Transactions on Education. 1999; **42**:33-38

[20] Hong H, Kinshuk. Adaptation to student learning styles in web based educational systems. In: Proceedings of World Conference on Educational Multimedia, Hypermedia & Telecommunications EDMEDIA. Lugano, Switzerland; 2004. pp. 21-26

[21] Paredes P, Rodríguez P. Considering sensing intuitive dimension to exposition-exemplification in adaptive sequencing. In: Proceedings of the AH2002 Conference. Malaga, Spain; 2002. pp. 556-559

[22] Zywno M. A Contribution to Validation of Score Meaning for Felder-Soloman's Index of Learning Styles, ASEE Conference. Nashville, Tennessee; 2003

[23] Felder R, Spurlin J. Applications, reliability and validity of the index of learning styles. International Journal of Engineering Education. 2005;**21**(1): 103-112

[24] Felder RM. Matters of style. ASEE Prism. 1996;**6**(4):18-23

[25] Paredes P, Rodriguez P. Considering learning styles in adaptive web-based education. In: 6th World Multiconference on Systemics, Cybernetics and Informatics. Orlando, Florida; 2002. pp. 481-485

[26] Hong H, Kinshuk D. Adaptation to student learning styles in web based educational systems. In: World Conference on Educational Multimedia, Hypermedia and Telecommunications. Lugano, Switzerland; 2004. pp. 491-496

[27] Stash N, Cristea A, De Bra P. Authoring of learning styles in adaptive hypermedia: Problems and solutions. In: World Wide Web Conference. NY, USA; 2004. pp. 114-123

[28] Martin E, Paredes P. Using learning styles for dynamic group formation in adaptive collaborative hypermedia systems. In: Workshop Adaptive Hypermedia and Collaborative Web-Based Systems (AHCW04), Web Engineering. Munich, Germany; 2004. pp. 188-197

[29] Deibel K. Team formation methods for increasing interaction during In-class group work. In: 10th Annual SIGCSE Conference on Innovation and Technology in Computer Science Education. Portugal; 2005. pp. 291-295

[30] Carro RM, Ortigosa A, Martin E, Schlichter J. Dynamic generation of adaptive web-based collaborative courses. In: Groupware: Design, Implementation and Use. Vol. 2806. Berlin, Heildelberg; 2003. pp. 191-198. LNCS

[31] Martin-Blas T, Serano-Fernandez A. The role of new technologies in the learning process: Moodle as a teaching tool in physics. Computers & Education. 2009;**52**:35-44. DOI: 10.1016/j.compedu.2008.06.005

[32] García-Peñalvo FJ, Conde MÁ, Alier M, Casany MJ. Opening learning management systems to personal learning environments. Journal of Universal Computer Science. 2011; **17**(9):1222-1240

[33] Romero C, Ventura S, García E. Data mining in course management systems: Moodle case study and tutorial. Computers in Education. 2008;**51**(1): 368-384

[34] Kumar V. An empirical study of the applications of data mining techniques in higher education. International Journal of Advanced Computer Science and Applications. 2011;**2**(3):80-84

[35] Castro F, Vellido A, Nebot À, Mugica F. Applying data mining techniques to e-learning problems. Evolution of Teaching and Learning Paradigms in Intelligent Environment. 2007;**62**:183-221

[36] Weng C-H. Mining fuzzy specific rare itemsets for education data. Knowledge-Based Systems. 2011;**24**(5): 697-708

[37] Romero C, Ventura S. Educational data mining: A review of the state-of-the-art. IEEE Transactions on Systems, Man, and Cybernetics Part C: Applications and Reviews. 2011;**40**(6): 601-618

[38] Mitchell TM. Machine Learning. India: McGraw-Hill; 1997

[39] Witten IH, Frank E, Hall MA. Data Mining: Practical Machine Learning Tools and Techniques. Burlington: Morgan Kaufmann Publishers; 2011

[40] Quinlan RJ. Generating production rules from decision trees. IJCAI. 1987;**87**: 304-307

[41] Rokach L, Maimon O. Data Mining with Decision Trees: Theory and Applications. World Scientific; 2014

[42] Vandamme J-P, Meskens N, Superby J-F. Predicting academic performance by data mining methods. Education Economics. 2007;**15**(4): 405-419

[43] Hssina B, Merbouha A, Ezzikouri H, Erritali M. A comparative study of decision tree ID3 and C4.5. International Journal of Advanced Computer Science and Applications. 2014;**4**(2):13-19

[44] Quinlan RJ. Improved use of continuous attributes in C4.5. Journal of Arti. 1996;**4**:77-90

[45] Breiman L. Random forests. Machine Learning. 2001;**45**(1):5-32

[46] Genuer R, Poggi JM, et al. Variable selection using random forests. Pattern Recognition Letters. 2010;**31**(14): 2225-1136

[47] Breiman L. Bagging predictors. Machine Learning. 1996;**24**(2):123-140

[48] Cano A, Leonard JD. Interpretable multiview early warning system adapted to underrepresented student populations. IEEE Transactions on Learning Technologies. 2019;**12**(2): 198-211

[49] Márquez-Vera C, Cano A, Romero C, et al. Predicting student failure at school using genetic programming and different data mining approaches with high dimensional and imbalanced data. Applied Intelligence. 2013;**38**:315. DOI: 10.1007/s10489-012-0374-8

[50] Márquez-Vera C, Cano A, Romero C, et al. Early dropout prediction using data mining: A case study with high school students. Expert Systems. 2016;**33**(1):107-124. DOI: 10.1111/exsy.12135/abstract